AF267425

Universe Within You

Jerimy Des

Paperback ISBN: 978-1-967828-97-5

Hardcover ISBN: 978-1-967828-80-7

Published by:
Pine Book Writing
www.PineBookWriting.com
R-10225 Yonge St, Suite #250, Richmond Hill, ON L4C 3B2, Canada.

Printed in the United States of America

Dedication

I wrote this book to inspire those who feel like someone made a mistake when they gave them life to push through the negative feelings, because the light is your guaranteed destination when you do.

Acknowledgement

I want to give thanks to the Creator for GIVING ME both the time, desire, and resources to complete this book.

Table of Contents

CHAPTER 1: FIRST THINGS FIRST

This book will help you reflect on and explore your emotions, guiding you in connecting with your feelings. Thoughts and feelings are linked because thoughts serve as the CEO, giving responsibilities to your emotional managers. I like to think of my body as a business building, with thought executives at the top and emotional workers on every level below.

I'm not here to impose my philosophies on you. I ask questions with the intention that you will engage with your thoughts interactively. There is a final question, near the end, that encapsulates the premise of this book: tapping into the Universe within you.

The Universe consists of subatomic particles, which include protons, neutrons, and electrons. These identical particles exist alongside our human bodies, and even though we can't see them, we can assume interactions occur between humans and the Universe.

It's fascinating how elements like the atoms inside us resemble planetary orbits in space, and how an image of a brain can look similar to our Universe when placed side by side. Scientists have identified the dark energy force, even though it doesn't interact with light; however, it exerts a gravitational pull that influences the Universe. Keep this in mind as we discuss both Light and dark energy forces. When I mention 'Force,' I'm talking about energy, and when I refer to 'Realm,' I mean the place where these forces originate.

You might have heard the terms Frequency and Vibrations before—they often describe how we connect and our environment. I won't get too technical, but remember that in physics, these are waves that carry energy within us. One of the most wonderful ways to experience Frequency waves is through music, which can influence our Endocrine and Autonomic Nervous System (ANS) with its Hz output. For example, listening to 528Hz music can help reduce stress, while rap music, which can reach up to 20,000Hz, can give an energizing boost during intense workouts.

As a disclaimer, I am not an author, nor do I ever aim to be one. To be considered an author, I would first need the desire to meet that definition, which I do not have or want. However, I am a writer who had an idea to write a book. That is all.

Though I attended college, I didn't attend a major university due to a 14 on the ACT and no college aspirations in high school. I believed education could lift me out of my low-income roots, so I pursued it actively. Serving honorably in the military opened educational opportunities. My mother loved me, and my father taught me determination, which I use to execute ideas, shaping my life's meaning.

I'm not sure what category to place this book in or what demographic it should appeal to, but I will say that if I have a strong enough desire to write this and you've found yourself reading it, then the Universe is working to bring us together. I do not possess some God-given talent that makes me a writer; I put the time into this craft, and that is all you need with any skill you want to learn.

Most books start with the author sharing their background, inspirations, and thanks. I believe the Higher realms of the Universe enabled this book's creation, so I thank them. My reasons for not revealing more about myself or my origins are not important here, as I want society to stop pigeonholing humans into categories.

I believe we often categorize people before talking to them, which naturally creates a divide. I encourage you to keep an open mind and be free of preconceptions, as this is the only way to truly hear and connect with what I'm saying in this book.

Emotional Pools

Throughout this book, I'll talk about emotional pools—both positive and negative. Think of using the positive emotional pool as soaring high in the sky like a plane, filling you with joy and energy.

On the other hand, tapping into the negative emotional pool is like driving through busy, congested roads below, which can feel overwhelming and stressful. Recognizing these differences can help us better understand our feelings and how they affect us.

Does Matter, Matter?

We've all heard about dark matter, but have you ever wondered about light matter? Does it really exist? Looking at it visually, yes, but physically, it often feels like the Sun is the only source nearby. Our bodies also absorb energy through feelings, and I've always been curious—where exactly do those feelings originate from?

The Pituitary Gland in your body is responsible for managing the energy from your food, but have you ever wondered what handles the energy when someone says something hurtful? Experts have pointed to the limbic system as a key part of your brain that manages basic emotions. This system helps regulate the autonomic nervous system, which controls your fight or flight response, as well as rest and digest functions. It does this by influencing the endocrine system, which releases hormones like adrenaline into your bloodstream, helping you respond to different situations.

I understand that might seem like a lot of scientific talk, but you may wonder how it relates to the dark matter I mentioned earlier. I bet that when you first saw this chapter and the words "Dark Matter," many non-scientists pictured a dark, floating rock in space.

Even now, scientists still do not fully understand what dark matter actually is.

Matter on Earth exists as solids, liquids, or gases. These states are made up of tiny particles called atoms and molecules. In a solid, the particles are strongly attracted to each other. They stay close together and vibrate in place, but do not move past one another.

In astronomy, dark matter is a fascinating and mysterious form of matter that doesn't seem to interact with light or electromagnetic fields. Its existence is suggested by gravitational effects that can't be fully explained by general relativity unless there's more unseen matter out there. On the other hand, atoms—mainly hydrogen, carbon, nitrogen, and oxygen—make up about 99% of the human body. Like matter and emotions, these atoms are invisible to the naked eye, reminding us of the many wonderful mysteries of the universe and ourselves.

Are you starting to understand how much the Universe is within you now?

Cool Brains

Ideas originate in the brain, where neurons produce concepts that require behavioral responses. Activities like watching adult videos or smoking weed can slow this process by reducing neuronal activity. I might sound like a '90s D.A.R.E. teacher from seventh grade, but these habits can weaken neural function. Still, it's worth noting that the marijuana plant was given a unique appearance and scent by the Universe, so that means someone saw the plant, felt good about it, started a fire, and with that fire, a good feeling overwhelmed them.

Take a moment to explore neurons, and you'll see how billions of them team up to send signals that help your body do all sorts of amazing things. For instance, when you decide to reach for a cold drink, neurons chat with your brain, letting it know your body could use some hydration. It might sound simple, but this incredible system keeps working seamlessly in the background, without you needing to think about it—unless you decide to pause it.

Sedating your brain's neurons, or pausing your brain's idea process, is more about knowing when it's the right time to do so. If you have a math quiz on Wednesday, but you smoke Tuesday morning and study that night, don't get mad at the Universe when you end up with a C.

The same concept applies to any thought you have because it's like turning your brain into an economy-class car instead of a luxury one. Imagine your thoughts as millions of green forest trees, and when you smoke or watch adult videos, it's not just a fire but a flood of water rushing over them.

Talking The Talk

One of the most significant indicators of your brain's functioning can be assessed through your manner of speech. Cultural differences in communication are identifiable by speech patterns; however, from a scientific perspective, have you ever considered that there exists an intelligent manner of speech correlated with the developmental capacity of the brain?

Growing up, I didn't speak much, mainly using language influenced by family and entertainers. I read more books, and my speech patterns began to change; I started to sound more 'white.' My cousin, who's from inner city Chicago, would make fun of me, but what he didn't realize was that my 'whiteness' was actually my brain's growth response to reading more, which showed in my improved communication skills.

Suppose you look at the dialects and accents across the British Isles among the early settlers of the United States. In that case, you'll notice similarities between them and certain regions in the American South. These folks from the British Isles didn't prioritize education when they came here, but they were still classified as 'white.' Even in Germany, southern speakers differ from those in the north, much like in the U.S., but what I'm talking about isn't just dialect — it's about communicative adaptation.

I once had the opportunity to meet the General Manager (GM) of a successful National Basketball Association team. People from my hometown might have thought he sounded 'black,' but what really stood out was that he was a lawyer who grew up in an affluent area in upstate Illinois. At some point in his life, he learned to adapt his communication style to connect with different kinds of people, which helped him succeed. Now, just imagine this same GM without his law degree—would he still be demonstrating intelligence by tailoring his speech to his audience, or should he revert to sounding like the 'white guy' he's often perceived to be?

Growing up in my neighborhood, a big part of my language was saying "you know what I'm sayin'" and using the word "n****." I was just adjusting to my environment. When I went to college, I faced some teasing, so I learned their ways and became a compelling speaker they had to listen to. The military was similar, and before I knew it, I was speaking like my leaders. Every culture has its way of communicating, but I believe that intelligent people master these styles to succeed better within different groups.

As I mentioned before, 'sounding white' is the colloquial way of saying you sound whitewashed in the black community. Still, as we elevate our thoughts, the frequency of intelligence is a combination of adapting while articulating the communication style you're adapting to. As we do this, our brain develops maps both consciously and subconsciously, which I call **Thought Lanes**.

CHAPTER 2: READING THE ROOM

In the last chapter, we discussed how you can adapt to your audience, but there are times when it just doesn't work. I once got invited to a party where I knew this attractive girl would be there, and I thought it would be a cool idea to talk about neuroscience; it didn't go so well, as you can imagine. In a situation like this, your frequency, or waves, needs to flow with the vibe, or else you want to be getting invited to any other parties.

Consider this: how would you connect with a room full of doctors with only a third-grade education? Or, how would a scientist fit in among social media influencers? From my experience, the only way to fit in is to approach with an open mind to learn from others. When people are in a teaching mode, and you adopt a deferential attitude, it creates a positive vibe.

Building connections can be challenging when you have the same level of knowledge as others, but asking questions in a friendly and casual manner is a great way to break the ice. It helps establish a warm and welcoming foundation for friendships because people enjoy seeing your growth journey—similar to following your favorite character in a movie, who often starts from humble beginnings and achieves great things by the end.

The World

When was the last time you had a little chat with your pet about tidying up the mess they made? Probably never, right? Humans usually communicate both verbally and nonverbally, but what really matters most is the feeling behind it. Often, people hold back from saying exactly what they mean because they want to protect the other person's feelings or, even better, avoid conflict.

Here's my friendly take on your analysis: It seems that a key, unchanging factor is that we will always be different, regardless of how many people there are. The part we can influence—the 'Y factor'—depends on how we choose to redirect our thoughts every day toward positive, inspiring ideas like innovation, creativity, and rewarding goals.

When we do this consistently, our brain's Reticular Activity System (RAS) tends to adjust to this new focus, making it our new normal. While negative thoughts such as biases, anger, despair, or jealousy often default to us, it's important to remember that we're not powerless against them. Over time, with effort, we can overcome these challenges and reach a better place.

After that last paragraph, I might just run for President! Just kidding. But really, ideas that come from the frontal and occipital lobes, while consciously calming thoughts from the amygdala, often inspire the desire to develop an idea and then work hard to turn your concept into a prototype that can generate profit, which is the foundation of starting any business.

This country (USA) is built on free enterprise. However, we also serve as an example for race relations worldwide, so I would hate for the person responsible for coming up with the next big idea (flying cars or a cure for cancer) to be sidetracked by negative thoughts that could lead them to homelessness or prison.

Information is our most valuable resource, created by our minds. Developing daily routines to shift our mindset can help unlock its full potential. If about 45% of people worldwide practice this, increasing that to 65% through daily reprogramming of each person's RAS could motivate collective efforts to develop skills that benefit the world—potentially eradicating incurable diseases like Amyotrophic Lateral Sclerosis (ALS) or allowing us to travel to other galaxies, as seen in movies.

This concept is a bit complex, but essentially, it involves replacing negative thoughts with positive affirmations, identifying your target skills, and sharing them with those who need or want them. This method can help resolve many issues, including ongoing conflicts, by conveying, "While I may not agree with everything about this person, I respect their skills and efforts, especially if they are highly skilled and working for me."

Your dormant idea is truly important. Take time now to think about what you enjoy doing the most that not only gives you positive feelings but also benefits those around you. This reflects your deep desire to develop a skill, but how do you plan to carry it out? Also, will you vote for me for President now?

Dream Realms

I once had a dream where I was in a unique clinic, unlike anything I'd ever seen, because it was filled with the most beautiful women. The strangest part was that I couldn't walk; I could only crawl. As I moved through the clinic, I suddenly realized it was a sex clinic that felt more like a brothel. Even though there were stunning women there, I knew I had to crawl out to protect something important: the energy vessel inside me.

While crawling around this clinic floor, I noticed two people talking in an open-door cubicle. I remembered a guy who looked like someone I'd seen leaving a strip club. He was trying to persuade a woman to do the right thing. Later, in this dream-like state, that woman, the man, and I found ourselves at a table reviewing a shady contract the clinic staff had just handed us. We all felt it was suspicious and quickly decided to leave, catching a bus that seemed to lead toward freedom.

Although I may not remember exactly who those individuals were, I genuinely felt that our subconscious minds brought together the energy of three real people within the same dream. Do you believe it's possible to be part of someone else's dreams through your subconscious thoughts and actions?

Dark Vs Light Energy Forces

Vibrations or feelings can enter your magnetic field with either low or high signals. For example, have you ever met someone and found yourself unable to stop smiling because you feel a good vibe whenever you see each other? On the other hand, if you work with someone you can't stand being around, or even if you're working remotely and they email you, it might be a good idea to take a break and give yourself some space!

Scientists have studied quantum entanglement involving sea corals, showing that particles can interact across any distance. Imagine a particle as a ball in Brooklyn, NY, bouncing at the same time as a ball in Los Angeles. These particles are tiny, smaller than atoms, called photons, and they carry Light Energy. Since this energy helps us see, it can also explain how we exchange energy with others. When you meet someone and feel an unfriendly vibe, it usually starts as a feeling, but is confirmed with a look. Think of the bouncing balls as a metaphor for your energy connection—if their bounce is synchronized, your energies are aligned; if not, it feels off, even if you can't quite say why.

Two massive energy sources in the Universe disperse energy: Light and Dark, or what movies and books have depicted as good versus evil. Photons act as carriers for these two primary energy sources, but choosing to draw from either depends on your own decisions as the Universe balances their struggle to gain the most energy.

At one point, I thought about channeling this dark or evil energy by calling an attractive girl ugly, intending to crush her ego built on social media likes and private messages telling her she was 'Miss It.' The more I reflected, the more I noticed beautiful women everywhere; it felt as though this opportunity was being handed to me. One night, when I saw a stunning girl walking through a supermarket parking lot, I rolled down my window and called her ugly. She looked at me as if she expected what I was about to say. I felt terrible afterward, so I decided to park and go inside the store to find her and apologize.

To my surprise, she was near the front entrance searching for kids' clothes. When I approached her, the most unexpected thing happened: she told me she could care less because she felt she had already anticipated someone saying something hurtful to her long before I arrived. I knew the Universe wouldn't forgive me for my apology to her, so within a week, someone called me something worse than ugly as the police got involved, and I was infuriated.

I was always told as a child to put into the Universe what I want out of it, and this was a perfect example of that. Because I consciously chose to enter a negative thought lane, the Universe prepared her subconscious reaction for me so I could actually feel the effect of being called ugly, not her. She was looking for things for her kid, which meant she was in a positive thought lane while I was driving in a negative one.

Let's remember what I mentioned about quantum entanglement and bouncing the ball in LA and New York. When someone draws their conscious thoughts from the universe's positive energy sources, good or even greater things tend to happen in return. On the other hand, if one taps into darker energies, unfortunate events will follow. It all begins with a conscious thought, which then leads to subconscious action from the **Universe's light or dark experience pools.**

It's crucial to pay attention to the last two paragraphs because your conscious choices—big or small—ultimately determine how the Light or dark energy forces influence your **subconscious experiences.** These forces take control of our lifespan, or what I call the **Life Stream**, and put us on autopilot toward their respective realms.

Primary And Sub Energy

Have you ever heard of the Nubile? Google defines this word: 1. (Of a young woman) sexually attractive, and 2. (Of a young woman) sexually mature; old enough for marriage. This definition, at face value, is innocent, but ask anyone who has experience with this word, and they will tell you that the everyday meaning of this word denotes a young woman working in the adult film industry.

So, how did the definition of this word evolve into something common folk would perceive to be sinister or taboo? My educated guess is that thoughts themselves draw from sub-energy fields, which draw primary frequencies of thoughts.

Words are broken down into Morphemes, Affixes, Prefixes, Suffixes, and Roots. Because the root of the word Nubile draws energy from the primary thought of sex, then the morphemes or more diminutive meaning of the word (young woman preparing for marriage) is nullified.

One could attest that marriage derives from pure Light Energy based on the collective frequency of our subconscious thoughts, but when a person says the word sex, it is opined as the most nadir element of love.

Later on, I will break down these primary and sub-energy fields in the form of our emotions. Although the internet has connected us in unimaginable ways, I will also discuss how the algorithm is being used by these primary and sub-energy fields to dictate our thought lanes.

CHAPTER 3: GETTING THERE

So, we've been discussing vibrations, thought frequencies, and energy sources, but now it's time to learn how to access them within seconds. I previously mentioned two massive energy sources in the universe, but the true answer lies in where and how I channel them. This process involves visualizing your inner consciousness by zooming into a visible energy source that makes you feel the absolute best. For me, it takes me back to moments when my friends and I were sitting outside, laughing after a basketball game, or when I returned home in eighth grade and my mother stopped me to congratulate me with $10 because I made the high honor roll.

The key is to concentrate on the exact moment and solidify that feeling, so you can summon it when necessary. It's not entirely clear why our brains tend to lean toward pessimism or worst-case scenarios, but this habit has significantly hindered progress in areas like flying cars or the spaceships from *Star Wars*. For example, the title *'Star Wars'* suggests advanced technology used primarily for conflict. Are we naturally inclined to engage in conflict?

The idea that ships are traveling through the universe is imaginary, but if we can see it, we can create it as a human race. I grab and harness energy from these two primary sources by stopping everything I'm doing and elevating my inner energy vessel through the universe, stopping in front of both, which look like two transparent square boxes the size of liquid oceans. They match the universe's appearance and look so close, but when I reach my hand out, they seem so far away as I float in front of them.

<u>Your Destination</u>

Your emotions guide you to these primary energy realms. For example, imagine you're a management executive at a local bank and have only been approving loans to a specific demographic. In that case, no one might notice, but the Universe interprets this as a negative emotion, causing dark energy subatomic particles to gradually start overtaking the energy vessel within you.

Imagine your body as an empty stick figure drawing on a piece of paper, with two crayons beside it—one light and one dark. This empty stick figure represents your energy vessel, and the two crayons are the energy sources I'm referring to. Now, imagine that at the end of your physical life on Earth, you will ascend and pass through either one based on which color has filled your stick figure the most. That's how the Universe will determine which realm has claimed your energy vessel.

So, if the management executive at the local bank took care of his family, was good to his wife, and was generally liked by the people who encountered him, how can his energy vessel still be won over by the dark energy realm because he ensured certain people couldn't get loans since he didn't want them in certain neighborhoods? Don't think about it too much right now because later I'll detail the answer.

Who Did You Vote For?

In ancient times, asking someone who they voted for might have been a casual conversation, but today, it has become as conflict-driven and polarized as street gangs. The dynamic between political parties triggers the same emotional response as opposing gang members because it fosters a sense of belonging based on shared morals and values. However, it also creates invisible, polarizing walls that hinder cooperation across sides. In physics, 'polarize' means to block or restrict the vibrations of a transverse wave, like light, either completely or partially in one direction. Since waves carry energy, being part of a group that offers a sense of belonging can also mean being exposed to darkness or subatomic particles that block light, filling you with negativity.

While politics should mainly focus on resource management and weekly explanations of tradeoffs, it often appears centered on racial issues. Could politics serve as a mask for underlying hatred among us? When I first moved to California, I stayed in Orange County. I didn't pay much mind to racial issues then because California felt like a place to explore my creativity—something I believed the Midwest lacked. It wasn't until I met locals from Los

Angeles County that I was warned about Orange County leaning toward one political side and its racial tensions, even though I didn't personally experience these issues there. As a Black man in Orange County, I dress well, speak respectfully, smile, and treat people with dignity and respect. In Inglewood, CA, I behaved the same way and received similar reactions. I met many men who, at some point, admitted to gang ties, which I respected as a reflection of cultural values from their background, similar to what I see in the Chicagoland area.

I started reflecting on the people in LA who mentioned Orange County to me, and questioned where the idea that hateful energy reveals politicians' true feelings originated. Before answering, have you ever thought about how you feel about the colors red and blue? Growing up, I never liked red. Now, I wouldn't say I love it either, but I often wonder why I feel this way and where this perception stems from.

My mother's favorite color is red, and she enjoys writing. You can see where my love for writing came from because you're reading this book, but why do I dislike red so much if it's her favorite? I invite you to think about your own relationship with colors. I suspect you'll recall a childhood memory that created a strong attachment to that hue. For me, I wanted a bike for my 8th birthday. Since my mom couldn't afford it, I cried all day. My aunt and older brother tried to distract me by pretending they bought a bike from the store. It was too small, so they had to return it before the store closed to get me a new one. Even though I never saw this bike, I believed them and stopped crying. When they supposedly returned from the store, I asked what color it was, and they said blue. I knew it was a lie to quiet my crying, but I kept dreaming of a blue bike. I talked about it often, and within a few months, I got that bike and loved every minute— including the time I was hit by a car while riding it, but I survived. A few years later, I had a red bike, which caused fights, accidents, and was eventually stolen. What does all this have to do with politics and gangs? It's all about shared experiences, not just good or bad, but the type of energy you gain from them that sets us in familiar emotional pools.

I'm not here to discuss politics, though, because if you think about it, it's all about resource tradeoffs. In California, visit Laguna or Newport Beach and observe how resources are allocated. Los Angeles shows a mix of homelessness, crude behavior, and luxury shopping. You can't judge intelligence based on per capita numbers in these areas or claim Orange County is better just because it looks nicer. The real issue is the widespread acceptance of how things are supposed to be.

I moved around a lot as a kid and liked some neighborhoods while disliking others. I remember driving to the East Side of my town when I was in seventh grade, and both my brother and I hated the school we attended on the first day. The East Side specifically had gangs that wore blue, but I still disliked being there because it didn't feel right. I never got into fights because I stayed to myself, but the energy was always off with the kids from the East Side. Even when I started high school, I wouldn't say I liked it because it wasn't the one I wanted to attend, and it was full of East Side kids. The high school on the West Side was my dream, and I often have dreams (and still do) of starting my senior year there with all my childhood friends.

Why didn't the universe let me attend the school I always dreamed of? I can only guess that I would have enjoyed high school, excelled in my classes, met the girl of my dreams, married her, and built the perfect family and life. It might sound like nonsense, but that was the life I envisioned. Since I didn't attend that school, my life has been filled with depression and misery. Do you feel sorry for me now? Regardless of your feelings, I'd say the chances of me writing this book were much lower because I didn't go to that high school. People say real growth happens when you're most uncomfortable, like forming gold.

Gold deposits form over millions of years through volcanic activity, erosion, and chemical reactions, making gold rare and valuable. I'm sharing this to help you see yourself as a rare natural resource, like Doré gold, which many overlook until it's purified into gold bars.

Men Vs Woman

Where does a man's power reside if a woman's power comes through her image? You might think this statement is silly, but if you like a single raunchy photo on social media, your algorithm will start showing you lots of half-naked *Virtual Sexcretaries*, either seeking your attention or money. Because of this, I want to stress that this will be the MOST IMPORTANT PART of this book, as it's the main reason I was able to write it, and more importantly, why you are reading it right now!

Sexual energy is the most powerful energy known to humans because it fuels other strong emotions. Think about this: you're single, working a typical job, and a new person starts—oh, and I forgot to mention, they're incredibly attractive. You've never really paid attention to your appearance, but you make changes to look more appealing to them, and suddenly, you're open to attending the after-work get-together.

Later, you discover that another person in your office shares the same interest in the new person, and now you feel competitive. What's even worse is that you find out that the new person has given their number to this co-worker, and they've been texting each other! The new person doesn't know that this co-worker was already involved with someone else in the office, so you find it within yourself to share the much-needed tea with the new person to make them aware. Was any of this necessary to admit that you were jealous and would do anything to undermine the competition, or were you just looking out for the new person so they won't get into the office orgy?

We all recognize how powerful sexual energy can be when we meet someone who draws it out of us. Social media provides a quick fix, but your emotions become intense when you meet someone face-to-face, look into their eyes, or enter their electromagnetic field, which acts like a super magnet to your energy. As a result, this energy sparks feelings of happiness, love, jealousy, anger, and joy. I used to go to this upscale gym mostly at night. The psychographics of gym-goers differ between morning and night, mainly due to age, although many younger people wake up early these days. At this gym, I'd always see a group of people, including two girls and three guys. The two girls had curves, and the three guys were aware of it, so they engaged in subtle nonverbal behaviors to provoke jealousy and emotion, and sometimes to annoy me, even though I didn't care. If I got irritated, it was because I was paying $300 a month for this gym while these guys were family members of the staff. I had two options: either switch to another time or confront these guys and risk getting kicked out, still owing a four-month bill. I chose the latter, even though I didn't want to, and started coming at different times, which really annoyed me. By the end of my membership, I returned to the night shifts, hoping to 'encounter' these guys again. To my surprise, one of the girls kept looking at me. I never acknowledged it, thinking it might be a setup to get me in trouble outside for "talking to her," but I did find it strange, especially since only two guys were with them, but now not working out together.

Within the last hour of my membership, the Universe granted me exactly what I wanted: I saw both girls and all three guys together, but they were all speaking softly, not laughing, and for some reason, they kept looking at me. This gym had two sections, and for some reason, I stayed on the side closer to the exit because it had the weights I liked to use. I usually did my run, then worked on my upper body, and then headed out, but since it was my last day and I wanted to confront this group, I went to the other side. To my surprise, the three guys had disappeared, leaving just the girls, but there was another girl there who was so beautiful I could tell she intimidated the other two girls, who usually looked the best among the other girls who also go late at night. I was so focused on the new girl that my anger vanished. Because these two girls noticed where I was looking, they positioned themselves by coming next to the same machines I was using and kept looking at me for validation. Instead of ignoring them, I nodded at one of the girls and moved to another machine. Her body language seemed to say, "Talk to me," but I was focused on taking in the new girl's information, which I did, and I still talked to her.

I wanted to share this story because your focus influences the emotions directed at you. I used the word 'cast' instead of 'throw' to show that these feelings are intentionally aimed at you. Imagine your emotions as colorful gel balls floating around an invisible shield. Green indicates joy; white, happiness; blue, gloom; red, anger; black, depression, and so forth. You can assign different colors if you like, but they represent your feelings. When someone captures your attention, your shield dissolves. They may not directly possess your emotions, but they can borrow many, keeping them from you. For example, if you have 100 Green balls and a family member passes away, those remain dormant in your shield. If your crush responds to your DM, 75 of them become active and bounce intensely inside your shield. These changes happen within your shield—balls only leave if someone takes them. Reflect for a moment on who or what you would want to take these emotions from your shield.

I want to take another look at social media and reflect on how it affects men and women who don't quite match the popular trends. As an average-looking guy who can only dream of dating someone who gets millions of likes online, I find myself experiencing subtle feelings of sadness sometimes, wishing for what I can't have. I also dated a girl who didn't fit the typical looks people often admire, so even though she was beautiful, she faced similar struggles. So, is social media mostly built on negative energy, or is it just certain apps? We might need to rethink whether we see the glass as half empty or half full. After all, any social media platform is created to bring us closer in ways we never imagined 20 years ago. The fact that millions of people with their unique personalities, languages, and cultures are out there is truly something to marvel at. That sense of wonder can keep us scrolling for hours. But I've noticed—if there are millions of people to explore online, why do I keep running into people in real life who've seen the same video?

Let's use 'Socialship' as a fictional name to represent the algorithm for all social media users. Since each deck has its own events, we can assume everyone on this ship knows these events occur; they just don't know the details until news spreads. Consequently, they choose to visit that deck instead of others to check it out. Everyone aims to reach the most lively deck, but along the way, they might get distracted and never arrive, or they might pause and meet someone on the bow while discussing having just attended the same event, witnessing the same person act goofy or get ejected. I use this analogy because it helps illustrate how the algorithm operates interactively. I once thought that major telecom companies arbitrarily set the algorithm to create thought lanes based on demographics to control our thinking, but that's far from the truth. They can't control individual phones, but they can manipulate marketing campaigns for sales data. Having met people from diverse backgrounds, I see that the algorithm isn't like multiple ships but functions as one. Like water seeking its level, it's a marketplace driven by supply and demand.

So, what does socialship have to do with the algorithm, and what are the implications of thoughts being directed at both men and women? It's simple: Sensual Energy drives social media because it has the highest demand. You and I both know that scrolling can last for hours because deep down, we want to see something provocative, and that's where the honest answer about where the energy you're drawing from lies. This becomes dangerous: There is an interactive relationship with the word demand. Socialship demands your attention by eliciting a specific emotion from you to set you on a certain path of thought or frequency. Because you are within that realm of thought or frequency, that's the exchange of energy you will experience when interacting with others in real life. For example, if your social media feed is filled with science or math videos, your energy will be aligned accordingly, so your real-life interactions will attract people with similar thoughts. Conversely, if you're watching a lot of X-rated content, you should expect to start interacting with people who are within that same frequency. This truly reflects how the Universe works because, believe it or not, your thoughts are connected to the Universe's experience realms that exist not only in space but all around us.

Sex Vs Love

Given the flood of sensual content we encounter these days, what truly sets genuine love apart from imitation? Having experienced real love, I can tell when something is just lust or pretense. I remember meeting someone who had all the qualities I desired, yet the feeling of love was missing. It wasn't there at first, but we started dating because we were both single and attracted to each other. By attraction, I mean external influences like videos and music that drew us together. I recall asking her if she watched "adult" content; she said she had, but had stopped, though I sensed she still watched them. Before meeting her, I was going through a period of abstinence, believing that avoiding "adult" content and 'self-love' would improve my chances of finding someone with genuine love. But that approach didn't work, and I will explain why.

When I was about 14 years old, I had a huge crush on a girl from high school who was Black. I only say she's Black because, as I mentioned before, external factors can influence attraction, and race is one of them when it comes to sex. Sex is part of love, but it isn't love itself. When I first made eye contact with her at age 14, I not only didn't see her as Black, but I also didn't care that she was a girl. I didn't wonder if she liked me because I was Black or because

I didn't have much money; I just felt something much deeper inside. Going back to the girl I mentioned earlier, I would look her dead in the eye and say I loved her, but we both knew it was a lie. We had good sex because she wanted a black guy, and I wanted a white girl — largely driven by the videos and music we consumed, which shaped our desires arbitrarily. Most of our sex talk involved themes of interracial relations we had seen in adult content, and that influenced us. But after a couple of months, this infatuation faded, and what we truly wanted from each other became the real motivation to either stay or move on.

With the internal factors now guiding us, our conversations turned to spiritual topics. On our way home from a trip, I played a song I knew she wouldn't appreciate. But how did I know she wouldn't like it? Because I sensed her disinterest in that type of music. I quickly tried to switch to a different song, but she wanted to clarify that she's agnostic. I'm not a devout churchgoer nor do I preach about God, but I am a Believer, and she isn't. When the topic of God arises, I understand the frustration—why would a higher power create people who look better than me, have more social media likes, greater talents, or a better life?

I lost my hair in my early 20s, and this made me more frustrated with God than anything else in my life. There isn't a time I go out without people cracking jokes. The anger I feel when people laugh at me from afar is beyond what you can imagine; I think I was ripped off in life, especially by God. So, if that's the case, why haven't I become an atheist or agnostic? I believe a man who's balding, short, or a woman who has no curves or isn't being called pretty & DM'd constantly has good reason to feel like God did us a disservice in this life. My choice not to send hateful energy comes down to one thing: I found a woman who feels the same way about me, and her feelings go beyond physical traits.

This woman wasn't exactly my usual type. She was shorter, had her own unique cultural background I'd never known before, and she was a mother of two. She was a few years older than me and wasn't in a traditional relationship, but she was living with a guy, and I just knew they were sharing a close, intimate bond. Despite all this, every time I saw her, including the very first time, I felt a mysterious feeling that can only be described as love. I was 23 at the time and had made a promise never to fall for someone with children, like my dad did. But as we started talking on the phone, after just a couple of conversations, it became clear we had discovered something rare — real love.

If you've ever felt true love for someone, it's like the energy in the room shifts so that you know they're there, and everyone can tell you have strong feelings for each other. She also naturally had qualities I loved about her, like being very clean and wearing perfume that was seductive to my pheromones, which made me want to be with her all night. Here's the kicker: this woman and I never kissed, had sex, or spent more than an hour together, but we both knew it was true love. Social media's rise has blurred the line of finding true love, but I have the solution.

True love feels like a fiery sensation similar to sex, but it involves the whole body reacting rather than just specific parts. I used to believe it came through eye contact, but I can't recall ever making eye contact with a woman and instantly feeling this burning sensation; I guess Ray Charles or Stevie Wonder would agree. If anything, women have made eye contact to show their interest, but 10/10, the feeling of love wasn't there through eye contact. Instead, if they felt anything, they would move closer to me but avoid eye contact. Earlier, I mentioned that I intentionally became abstinent to find that feeling of love more clearly. However, it didn't work out, and I kept asking the Universe why I didn't experience that feeling of love when I was doing everything right. So, what was really happening?

When you don't masturbate, you initially feel very productive, especially for men. This lasts about a week before anger surfaces, and you might want to release frustration. I once dated someone who said the same. Many believe masturbation is a sin, and if you think sex outside marriage is wrong, it's hard to see its natural benefits.

During abstinence, I focused on avoiding sexual thoughts and often went to bed with a throbbing sensation. Despite attending online school, by day's end, I needed either to be with a woman or release it myself because I wasn't financially stable — I had to do it alone.

If I were doing everything right, why didn't the Universe give me a temporary girl to keep me motivated? It comes down to where the Universe needs you to be rather than where you think you should be. I have found real love, but even as I write this, I haven't been allowed to be physical with a woman I truly love. The thing is, if you're reading this book, please understand I wouldn't have written it if I was physically involved with someone I genuinely love because I wouldn't have the motivation to write. I am good at writing because I have the motivation, but I'm not naturally motivated to write a book, so the Universe made sure I would write this book with the plan to find real love so we can be as physical as we want. I suggest staying away from adult content, music, and similar stuff because, in the next chapter, they can steer you away from where the Universe needs you to be.

<u>Hate Love Affair</u>

I believe it's helpful to understand what the word "Pontificate" means before we continue. Before I learned this word, I always valued my own opinion on every topic because I see myself as the main character in my story—that's just natural. But have you ever thought about what role you play in other people's stories? For example, the bully who teased you in grade school or the girl who took your boyfriend—probably they're the villains in your story. But do you ever wonder if you have a part in theirs? "Pontification" is about sharing your opinions and judgments from your own very biased perspective—you see things through your own eyes. When you send out positive or negative energy, would you say you genuinely love who you are or dislike parts of yourself? Take a moment now—find a mirror where you can see most of your body, look into your eyes, and ask yourself: 'Do I love myself or do I struggle with myself?'

The first time I did this, my eyes teared up. I pointed out the imperfection—guessing I looked worse, living alone as a single guy with no love interest, and that I am a waste—but didn't hate myself. I was more upset with my past actions or inactions, but could accept my reflection. This isn't about self-help or improving, but about measuring where your thoughts draw energy from.

I realized that my negative thoughts stemmed from dark energy, and they needed to change immediately. Within that same hour, I looked into the mirror, stared into my eyes, and declared that I was the greatest. I smiled and turned off the lights. The following weeks were remarkable because I began drawing from Light Energy, and those around me noticed the difference.

Before this shift, I often practiced "self-love" by telling myself how awful I was, believing it was the reason no girls were interested in me. This was misguided thinking. Many single women also engage in self-pleasure, so why should that matter? I reassured my subconscious every time I engaged in this practice, and whether it was true or not, it helped me maintain a positive mindset on those days. On days I didn't, I simply reversed my thoughts.

What I'm doing here is manipulating both my subconscious and conscious thoughts, allowing my neurotransmitters to send positive signals to my body, which is now fueled by Light Energy.

A person can be an adult film content creator but still draw from Light Energy, or a preacher can stand on the pulpit every Sunday, drawing from dark energy. This might seem absurd to a very religious person, so stop reading if that's how you feel, but I ask you to hear me out because I'm concerned about feelings and their connection to the two main energy sources.

I respect religious organizations and those seeking spiritual growth. I introduce the idea of drawing from light or dark energy. I believe in God, as Earth's oceans and trees' oxygen production are unexplainable without divine help. Many feel negative about God, leading to curses and bad outcomes linked to those thoughts. Consequently, the entity known as God has evolved to adapt to modern tactics influenced by the dark energy force.

What does this evolution involve? For instance, a former adult content creator later became a lawyer, dedicating herself to help free men who are wrongfully imprisoned. While she may not be perfect, has she made a bigger impact by inspiring people with her positive energy and actions, which have touched billions of fans? Another interesting idea is that the Universe might be shifting the names Lord/God & Heaven to more modern terms like Light Energy Force, to help ease any fears connected with traditional names.

By now, you might be considering or have already reflected on how my thoughts fit within one of the major organized religions. Pantheism is the belief that the Universe itself is a Deity. You could imagine that if God is Omnipresent, He might be as vast as the Universe or as tiny as a tick, and He could even be a She, existing at the same time! I won't bore you with a history lesson on Pantheism and its origins, but I encourage you to think about how organized religion has influenced your perception and connection to these energy forces.

Growing up, my mother made sure we attended church regularly, and despite our efforts, we sometimes strayed from what the religion considers the 'Word.' As I got older, I found myself drawn more to the Islamic faith, inspired by how the women behaved and carried themselves. When I began visiting the Mosque, I felt a sense of being on the right path. However, everything changed when I started developing feelings for a female member; I soon realized I was culturally inexperienced with Arab customs and traditions.

I started to wonder whether I was there to serve God or to find a wife so I could serve God fully. I was afraid that if I asked the elders whether she was dating someone, I might be silently ostracized for my true reasons for going to the Mosque, so I stopped going. Years later, I returned to organized religion, this time to a church, and honestly said I felt more at home there. This church was mostly Nordic, unlike the church I grew up in, and I felt a sense of kinship like never before.

I've always been comfortable around different cultures. Still, I enjoy being with these people most because they are less judgmental, liked how I spoke, and made it feel acceptable to date one of their relatives. Yes, I said they were okay with me dating a relative.

Was I just the token black guy who fetishizes certain types of girls late at night? I admit I think about them during those hours, but the idea of fetishization seems absurd to me. I needed to understand the sensual chemistry I felt and its origins. Don't misunderstand, the first girl I ever fell in love with was black, but her rejection led me to explore connections with girls who were interested in me.

I once dated a biracial girl who could pass for a Latina. She was beautiful and had all the curves, but I felt nothing when we kissed. After her, I dated a Black girl, and I had the same empty feeling when I kissed her. Then, right after her, I dated an Asian girl, and I still felt nothing.

I'm almost certain that none of these girls genuinely felt a connection for dating, but they agreed since I was paying for all the dates, and I wasn't unattractive. Although they come from different backgrounds, they all, at some point, hinted or implied that I favored white women. But how would they know if I never showed or admitted this to them?

People receive their instincts or intuition about the type of person they're meant for or who others are attracted to from a form of collective Universal energy that lies dormant within our subconscious experiences. The problem is that we haven't instinctively broken free from these negative emotional pools of thought.

So, if you're not involved with who you want to be with, can you honestly be drawing energy from the Light side of the Universe? The simple yet hard truth is that you are not, because jealousy is one of the many subset energies coming from the dark energy force. Some people genuinely don't have a preference and want to find love, and they will at some point; these types of individuals are drawing from Light Energy.

Some people, like I once was, resemble what I would call '*Adolfs*.' They deny themselves the pursuit of finding someone they truly wish to be with, embarking instead on a personal journey that spreads the dark energy they harbor. This destructive path often stems from their failures, leading them to view life through a distorted lens fueled by negativity. A close examination of Dictator's past often reveals unrequited love for a person that leads to their transformation into a monster.

I've dated many women because we share similar cultural values, but ultimately, you either have this vibe with someone or you don't. The vibe I'm talking about is an unspoken, rare feeling that just happens naturally, and when it does, you instantly share it with that person without needing to say a word.

The longest relationship I had lasted eight months. After six months, she would call me in the middle of the night and tell me he had a dream about me being with this girl who looked nothing like her, but we both knew deep down we didn't have that unexplained feeling for each other.

I felt anger toward the Universe because she was right, and her feelings started to drift away from me after that. I asked for this rare vibe or feeling from her, but it never materialized, even though I believed she was perfect for me and that our relationship would have had less conflict in the eyes of the public.

Although she appreciated my skills in the bedroom, it frustrated her that I wasn't progressing toward meeting her at the goal line because the problem was that she wasn't the girl she had dreamed of me being with. I realized the answer might lie within the gay population.

Gay Energy

I think it's hard to tell people what your dating preferences are because you can't predict who you'll have a vibe with when you meet them, but I understand the idea behind it. I once made a list of women I instantly felt a vibe with, and to my surprise, they all had different skin tones. Furthermore, I wrote down their body shapes, and it also did not show the same "figure." The only thing they had in common was the fact that they were all women.

Gay people hold a special place in the realm of sensual energy because conservative organized religion often struggles to explain this anomaly without associating it with some past abuse they experienced.

I've met many gay people in the past who never experienced such trauma but knew from an early age what they liked based on the vibes they received from the Universe. Moreover, a lot of the gay people I know emit their interconnected energy without saying a word. In my opinion, gay people have the most accurate form of sensual energy because if they deny it, their lives will undoubtedly suffer.

A gay person's sensual nature is like the formation of a diamond. Diamonds contain the same subatomic particles as atoms, but in greater numbers due to the pressure they endure during formation. Gay people feel the same kind of pressure from conservative organized religions. So, should gay people ultimately give up on attending worship at venues associated with organized religions, or should they create their own organized religions and worship among themselves, with these organizations being seen as sects of the dark energy force?

If they do so, which venue is providing the correct primary energy source? I do not have the answers to those two questions, but I can say that it all depends on the source from which the energy originates. The Church of Latter-day Saints and Islam follow different doctrines; however, when interacting with their sincere followers, one can only commend their pursuit of righteousness, which is rooted in Light Energy and its related energies.

Love Vs Lust

Having spent nearly four decades on Earth, I've realized how society's perceptions have influenced who I am—even before I was born. I share this because I am seen as a Black man living in America, as an American. I used to highlight gender and race differences when I was younger, but I wonder if this way of thinking might seem a bit sexist or racist, as if I'm implying the Universe specifically chose these traits for my energy vessel for my purpose, rather than for its own.

Isn't it intriguing how simply mentioning 'black' and 'white' can stir intense emotions? Consider that when we say these words, we now understand how they should be perceived. Imagine if everyone had the opportunity to make a deal with the Creator before entering this world.

They might choose what they believe is good, only to realize there's no turning back once they're here. It's natural for some to wish to look or be celebrated like actor Brad Pitt or the famous artist Beyoncé — everyone has their own desires. And here's another curious thought: would you ask the Creator to enhance your intelligence today if it meant accepting a tradeoff in your appearance? It's a truly intriguing question to think about!

In typical Black American culture, appearance and how others see you often overshadow accomplishments such as higher education; this is also true in Hispanic culture. Although many people within these communities are well-educated, the common attitude usually emphasizes looking attractive first and then concentrating on intellectual endeavors.

I understand that statistics can be quite dull, and they get old, so I'll skip over that. However, when it comes to social algorithms, sex appeal from any demographic is winning the algorithm over every other topic.

Just like globalization, where some countries sell specific products to the world market to sustain their livelihoods, different cultures offer dominant appeals that enrich our overall human emotional well-being. Because social media presents the full range of these cultures, the most appealing ones are the most discussed, which is often when topics like sexism and racism emerge.

I would say I love my race, but does that make me a racist? Some argue I can't genuinely love my race if I prefer girls who are not black. However, as a black man living in America, it might be socially acceptable to say I love being black because society subconsciously recognizes this sentiment. But for a buddy of mine who happens to be white, grew up in the same neighborhood, and shares the same values, saying he loves his race isn't understood the same way, both consciously and subconsciously.

We understand the everyday meaning of what my white friend and I are saying, but why is there just a material difference between two different people saying the same words? History influences this, but what if the black guy sounded white and the white guy sounded black? I know some readers will say sounding white or black is ridiculous, but what I'm saying is vernacular, and that concept is generally understood. So, if it's generally understood that a white guy who sounds black has a higher chance of dating a black girl, while a black, who sounds white is a better fit at the corporate table, opposed to the security desk.

I remember meeting a young Hispanic woman at a Southern California bar, and one of the first things she pointed out to me was that, based on how I sounded, she would have guessed I was "whitewashed." I had heard this term before, but it had never been directed at me. A few months later, this Hispanic girl confided in me that she did feel a good vibe between us, but she wanted to have children with a white guy because she didn't want her kids to be darker than she was. Here I am, a Black guy, listening to her as she lay next to me in my bed, and for some reason, I accepted this because I understood how society had shaped her subconscious to influence her conscious choices.

Did I think she was racist? Not at all, since we had strong chemistry. However, her preferences and my acceptance are part of the Universe's plan to balance two forces. The Pantone Skin Tone Guide, a top authority on color standards, identifies 138 human skin tones. So, why is society conditioned to emphasize these subtle differences? Furthermore, if slavery and eugenics had never existed, would society have paid less attention to these distinctions? It's all due to the Universe's attempt to balance the energies of light and dark.

CHAPTER 4: THE GREAT EMOTIONAL DIVIDE

Have you ever wondered why children are continually taught to choose what is right over what is wrong? If the Universe and its Creator were genuinely benevolent, creating a seemingly Utopian world, then why does the world often appear to be in chaos? Why do we seem to thrive on conflicts in politics, gang culture, Walmart versus Target shoppers, and other divisions like blue versus red that occur everywhere in society?

Instead of two people trying to figure out why they both love ice cream so much, it's more about exploring what motivates your choice to live in Arizona instead of Illinois. I understand how important it is to belong to something that reflects a big part of who you are and how you think. Depending on which group you identify with, it's natural to see the other side as different or even misunderstood.

So, if you feel like you're drawing from Light Energy, what are those specific emotions, and how do they differ from what your Opps are drawing from? Before we explore that, understand that there is a scientific connection between you and the universe, since the human body's main chemical elements—hydrogen, oxygen, carbon, and nitrogen—are also found in the universe.

The body's limbic system is the main center for emotions, with only 27 distinct emotions. Because there are only these 27 emotions,[1] they process feelings based on past, present, and future experiences. Here are the body's set emotions:

- Admiration

- Adoration

- Aesthetic appreciation

- Amusement

- Anxiety

- Awe

- Awkwardness

- Boredom

- Calmness

- Confusion

---

[1] Cowen, A. S., & Keltner, D. (2017). Self-report captures 27 distinct categories of emotion bridged by continuous gradients in a semantic space. Proceedings of the National Academy of Sciences, 114(38), E7900-E7909.

- Craving

- Disgust

- Empathetic pain

- Entrancement

- Envy

- Excitement

- Fear

- Horror

- Interest

- Joy

- Nostalgia

- Romance

- Sadness

- Satisfaction

- Sexual desire

- Sympathy

- Triumph

Many people believe there are thousands of emotions, but in reality, countless experiences are linked to these 27 emotions. For example, if you and I walk into a bank at the same time, we might say hello, both recognizing the feeling of getting paid. However, if I go there to secure a loan and you pull out a few thousand dollars to shop on Rodeo Drive, the look we exchange as we walk in will feel very different. Still, if we enter and my balance is $200 while yours is $20 million, but the place gets robbed, we will share the same emotional experience for a lifetime, regardless of our financial status.

None of these emotions are directly linked to the Light Energy or dark energy realms. However, since the Universe allows both realms to draw on your energy to grow, they transmit subatomic particles through elements in your environment from the moment you're born to influence your emotions, causing the chaos I mentioned earlier.

If you notice, Love is not on this list because it's not an emotion but a collection of these emotions. On the other hand, Hate is also not listed, but we all know what emotions are involved with this word. If hate represents dark energy and Love represents Light Energy, why is it so hard to determine who's drawing from what? The answer lies in your feelings because feelings reveal the true emotional sensation you're experiencing in real-time based on the pool of 27 emotions. These 27 emotions are the sub-energies I've been referring to.

Remember earlier, we talked about how the Universe and our bodies share the same particles? These particles are essentially chemical compounds found both within us and in our surroundings. Smart stuff, but I just want to highlight how humans exchange chemicals with their environment, facilitating stronger connections with others who share similar experiences. For instance, if I've been watching funny videos and then decide to go to the gym, I'm likely to want to connect with someone who has done the same, because the Universe creates invisible pathways of particles for people who think alike.

What do these invisible pathways of particles carry, and what do they look like? If you look through a telescope and imagine seeing the right side with dark source energy while the other side has light source energy, with millions of threads reaching from Earth to both of them, that's the best way I can describe it. These particles can attach to people, places, or things.

Now, think about where you work; for the most part, you can tolerate the people there because your basic needs are met, but have you ever gone to a place you usually visit at a different time and felt like the energy was off? What about that bar you thought felt weird before, and now you have the scars to prove it?

My town had two gyms: one eleven miles away and another five miles away. I usually chose the eleven-mile gym because I felt more comfortable going there. I avoided the five-mile gym because of negative feelings. One night, despite my discomfort, I went to the closest gym, and nothing happened. However, on the third night, I got into a conflict and never returned. This gym seemed to draw from a negative energy source, but we'll discuss that later.

As I stated, we have 27 emotions, which are processed feelings based on past, present, and future encounters or experiences. Because the particles in and around us are not subject to time constraints and can travel almost as fast as the speed of light, one can only assume that they not only carry the experiences attached to our emotions, but also if those experiences gravitate toward certain pools of emotions.

Each emotional pool, whether positive or negative, activates based on our feelings or sensations and creates an invisible particle link to either light or dark force energy sources. These particles, according to Chaos Theory, can move freely within our ecosystem, producing images at both conscious and subconscious levels to influence us toward either side. For example, you might wonder why some of your dreams feel like silent movies, with familiar faces that evoke different emotions. These particles are using your thoughts to trigger emotions that benefit either side, creating invisible pathways toward one or the other.

People always say, "Read the room." Well, this is your ability to mentally scan your own emotions against the universe's existing emotional particles (i.e., energy) to see which path you're on in real time. Once again, these particles carry the past, present, and future experiences attached to our emotions, enabling us to communicate verbally or non-verbally with those who have experienced the same feelings, regardless of time. What this means is that the particles will indefinitely present images to your mind, but if you allow these particles to also influence your emotions, you can feel the same feelings of hate from 100 years ago as if it is happening right now!

What I shared with you is the formula for connecting to the collective consciousness of the Universe. For instance, if a man watches a lot of adult videos and expects to meet a girl, he's likely to encounter either a girl who also watches adult content or a real adult content creator. Unfortunately, both of these individuals are drawing from dark energy rooted in their emotional pools.

If someone genuinely seeks Love, a collection of positive emotions, they should begin to draw from Light Energy emotions, encouraging the Universe to guide them along those emotional paths. This will increase the likelihood of a love connection forming. To all singles longing for happiness, I urge you to focus intensely from now on, as the Universe emits only 27 emotions, making it easier for you to follow either path.

What's Love Got To Do With It

So, what is love if it's not one of the 27 emotions? Love is truly a beautiful journey through your past, present, and future experiences with someone special. When I made the move out west to California, I noticed the energy shift among my family and friends because our experiences changed due to the new environmental chemicals I was exposed to. One of the most uplifting feelings I've had was relocating to California to chase my dreams in screenwriting; many back home couldn't quite understand. Even after arriving in California, I found ways to connect with the locals because, although the screenwriting dream was a bit blurry, I knew they understood because, well, it's California.

Visiting the Santa Monica Pier, I experienced a dream-like atmosphere, feeling it as a hub of shared thought chemicals that hold past, present, and future emotions connected to our feelings. It's like a space where paths enable us to communicate, both verbally and non-verbally, with others experiencing similar emotions in real-time. In essence, this is how people fall in and out of love: their thought energy either aligns and stays connected or conflicts, leading to breakups.

You might feel regretful if you claim to have been in love only once. However, because you understand how to manage your emotions and keep them aligned with your partner's, your second love will be more remarkable, as you know how to nurture and sustain love. I'm not suggesting you should abandon your first true love. Instead, what I'm sharing is the formula for maintaining attraction.

There are many resources explaining what attraction is and the laws involved. I encourage you to explore those, but here I want to focus on the maintenance aspect of attraction. I've dated many women who initially put on a great show when we first met, including myself. However, once we move in together and face our first disagreement, the question of attraction naturally arises for both of us. It is often said that strong relationships endure through effective communication. From a maintenance or technical perspective, this communication is about assimilation—maintaining the same emotional connection frequency.

If I secretly admire a risqué Social Media model while dating someone, I start to draw dark energy through aesthetic appreciation, causing my emotional frequency to shift away from her. Meanwhile, she might want me to draw Light Energy from romance; our connection won't last very long.

Both women and men have 27 emotions, so it's not accurate to say one is more in touch than the other. These emotions have existed for centuries, and understanding them can drastically improve your skills in math, emotional intelligence, or anything else. Women express emotions through courses, books, and support for self-growth. Ten years ago, that idea sounded ridiculous; in my upbringing, being in touch with emotions was seen as soft. Reflecting on my "harder' self, I drew from dark energy, evident in the people around me. Thankfully, the Universe can place you in environments that draw from dark energy, allowing you to become a beacon of light.

Many people understand the casual meaning of "toxic" in relationships, but often they remain unaware that they are tapping into dark energy. We tend to visualize a toxic person based on exaggerated portrayals in movies and TV, yet sometimes these individuals are so subtle that it's hard to recognize them. I had a childhood friend with whom I was close for years until I moved to California; gradually, their quiet comments began affecting my feelings. It wasn't that their words were outright negative—more that they made me feel uncomfortable, causing me to scrutinize the tone rather than the content. They were a good person, so why did I detect this subtle emotional shift between us now?

As a screenwriter, one of the first lessons in creating a compelling story is mastering subtext. Subtext involves expressing your true meaning without explicitly stating your desires. For instance, if you're interested in a girl at the gym, you wouldn't directly say, "I like you." Instead, you might comment, "I always see you here working hard." This approach taps into a range of emotions, fostering a positive connection. Essentially, maintaining a healthy relationship involves doing and saying things that evoke positive feelings, which in turn draw energy from a source of light and positivity.

Growing up in challenging neighborhoods with modest homes, we moved frequently. Despite the upheaval, my mom always diligently cleaned and sterilized each place, creating a positive atmosphere rather than dwelling on our hardships. She never spoke negatively about any of our homes. By focusing on calm, Light Energy, she taught us to draw from that same positivity, even in places others might see as dark. Today, some family members sometimes bring up those difficult times, but they are typically shut down because preserving your energy from negativity is vital. Sometimes, that means stepping away from those trying to pull you into darker emotions.

I previously mentioned that the Universe guides you on these Universal Pathways based on your thoughts; this is important because it reflects your current path. I love rap music, but a subgenre called Drill often discusses the imbalance between you and your Opposition (Opps). Drill gives me a feeling of supreme confidence but also a sense that I can confront any negative opposing energy with the same fury, allowing me to draw from the Light Energy of triumph. Yet, somehow, it also puts me on a dark energy pathway. Confusing, right? Let me explain this better.

Growing up surrounded by gang activity, I could have followed that path and drifted away from society, but I chose to channel that intensity into my studies and work toward a college degree. Later in life, I realized that many creative individuals also draw on similar dark energies as a source of inspiration. I earned two of my three college degrees by transforming that dark muse into motivation, often believing that others didn't see the intelligence I possessed. I used to think that Black people were perceived more as trendsetters rather than for valuing education. In America, it's common to see stereotypes where a Black, White, or Asian person is judged based on who's seen as the most brilliant leader or whose 'cool' stereotypes fit. These stereotypes really upset me. They become even more pronounced when comparing roles like an Engineer, a Rapper, and an Entrepreneur. All of this fueled a strong feeling of frustration in me!

Many people view gangs negatively, but I want to explain how they can contain a mix of light and dark energy that ultimately guides them toward the Light Realm. Gangs foster a sense of kinship and confidence, providing access to feelings of positive energy. These positive emotions can also help overpower negative feelings during tough situations. This is similar to the energy experienced when being part of the Red vs Blue political divide, except it can escalate to violence with rivals. When thoughts of harming or killing opponents influence actions, it indicates that the subconscious experience is now drawing from dark and negative emotional pools. While I do not condone gangs, I believe that someone raised in that environment can, with awareness of potential deadly, homeless, or prison outcomes, harness this blend of energies—light and dark— toward what society deems productive.

Conscious Vs Subconscious Minds

Growing up in a low-income, impoverished area, I learned that focusing on positive emotions can shield you from those caught in darker thoughts. Poor neighborhoods across America are filled with people from diverse backgrounds, but often, their emotions are overlooked. Many successful individuals living in wealthier areas originated from these challenging environments, and they succeeded by tapping into positive energy subconsciously. It might seem contradictory that I used 'dark energy' to earn my degrees, but that was my way of navigating a tough journey. Imagine myself on a train in a dark tunnel, with the light at the end — the destination was always to see the light or sky.

At this point, you should understand that if the conscious mind is the GPS destination and the subconscious represents the routes, then making pathway choices becomes much easier. I used to think the same, but in real-life situations, you need to use reverse engineering to understand how your brain's neurotransmitters connect to the Universe. Just like the Universe, your mind has mapped every experience you may encounter.

With countless experiences mapped out, the Universe ultimately guides us to two primary destinations: the Light Realm or the Dark Realm, which represent your conscience. Since many paths can lead to these destinations, you navigate your subconscious daily. For instance, I chose to write 500 words each day to complete this book instead of browsing social media and potentially stumbling upon inappropriate content. My attraction to such content doesn't determine my energy source; rather, it is the choices I make that influence my subconscious pathways.

Many beautiful and curvaceous women struggle to find love because of the wide range of positive and negative emotions they and those interested in them experience. When a person has to draw from a balance of the 27 emotions, it often overwhelms their subconscious; I call this rare anomaly within the Universe's thought realm a *Lythmyrthle*. The Lythmyrthle is a puzzle because you don't know if your subconscious is drawing energy from the Light or Dark Realms. If the Universe only sets two GPS destinations, the Light and Dark Realms, how does one decode the trillions of mapped-out experiences to reach them? In response to helping us navigate these destinations, the Universe produces guides for either. I started looking at guides like the Bible, Quran, and Torah to reach the Light Realm, but my emotional response isn't always driven by Light Energy.

Furthermore, the argument against following these guides is that the universe may have already preset many of our paths for either the Light or Dark realm. If I'm born with a deformity like going bald early and most women find me unattractive, I will unquestionably be drawn from the dark energy source. If I look at someone like Joel Osteen, who teaches from the biblical guide, I would argue that his ability to draw toward the Light Realm is much easier than mine because he doesn't have that bald deformity to contend with. It's safe to say that the unattractive girl with no curves or a parent whose child was born disabled has justifiable negative emotions. The fact that they're predisposed to a life leading to the Dark Realm because of the negative feelings they're forced to draw from makes you wonder why the subconscious mind exists.

I never thought I'd become a fan of someone like Joel Osteen: a southern white man who grew up middle class, had a full head of hair, and found love with his beautiful wife early on. I've always struggled with the idea of God for the reasons I mentioned earlier, and I'm not part of any organized religion. Still, when I first heard him speak, he sparked so many positive feelings in me that I couldn't ignore him. I subconsciously wondered, "I don't want to feel good when I listen to this guy, so how is he doing it?"

At that time, I was homeless, living out of my car, balding, and without a love interest. I remember gazing at the sky and imagining the large rocks scattered across it. This led me to think of Mr. Osteen and the guides describing a perfect realm where everyone is attractive and all children are flawless. That night, as I observed the dark, scattered masses, I realized I had hit a low point in life by letting the particles of darkness slowly consume my mind, and the universe indicates only one place free from negative feelings: The Light Realm.

Believing in a place you've never seen can be quite challenging. Many people have shared stories of the Light realm, calling it heaven, and some have even dreamt about it. But not many have actually traveled there and come back to tell us exactly how to get there. Do we need to go through hardships here to reach it? I want to share that I believe the Light realm exists; for me, setting a goal to reach a place where negative feelings no longer hold power over me has made a big difference. When I focus on what others might have or lack, I tend to invite darker energies.

I guess knowing that I didn't have a choice about any of the physical traits I was given when I entered this world fresh out of my mother's oven never gave me a sense of entitlement. Now, if I was born and taught entitlement based on how I look and what I have compared to others, that would have changed me, but I don't have those words to write. What I do know and can write about is living a life where I mostly feel positive feelings that will attract the attention of the Light Realm.

Before we proceed, take a look at Figure A as we explore these emotions within the Categories and Subcategories of Love and Hate.

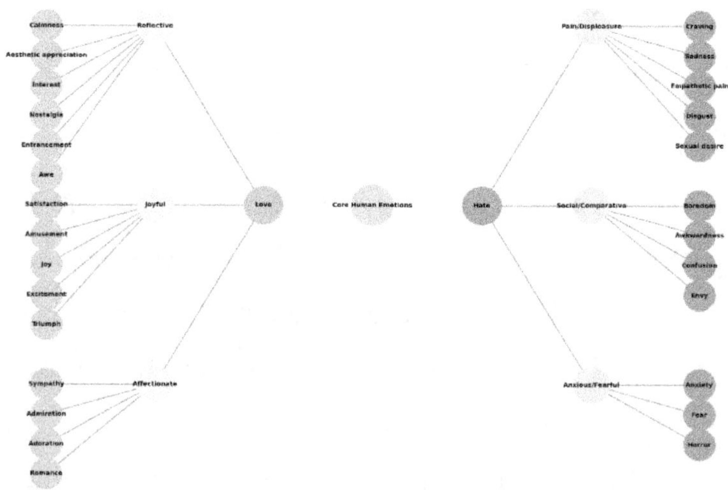

Figure A

<u>This Ish Is Biblical</u>

My mother did a great job of taking my brothers and me to church so that we knew the right things to do in life. I don't remember anything the preacher said to me as a child that brought me closer to believing in the concept of God. By the time I got to high school and realized how much poorer I was than the other kids, I became agnostic and started skipping school to avoid the comments and snickers about my clothes. During that time, I had no positive emotions to draw Light Energy from because my feelings were always negative. Many of the guys I got along with felt the same way as me, but they were dropping out of school to do things to make themselves feel better, and by that, I mean getting money the fast way.

One thing I can proudly admit is that I have never sold drugs. The reason I never sold any drugs is because I saw the effects drugs had on both of my stepfathers. One got his leg shot over a drug deal, and the other stole anything valuable from our house just to sell it. I remember around 1997, we got a computer from my mom's coworker, and he stole and sold it. Imagine seeing little kids play on a computer, but you're not thinking of the joy it gives them; you're just thinking about how much you can get from it to boost your own dopamine. This was just one of many incidents, but his choices eventually led him to become completely consumed by the dark energy force. For me, witnessing all of this, I didn't want anything to do with it.

Furthermore, it was the early 2000s, and we'd visit suburban areas where the American dream seemed to unfold, only to have the police called on us. Back then, I didn't see myself as a poor Black guy from the hood; I believed that if I worked hard, I could achieve that American dream. But, boy, was I gullible!

After honorably serving in the US military, I transitioned to civilian life by going to school and landing a good job. In those early months working in corporate America, I truly felt I was on my way to achieving the American dream, surrounded by wonderful people. I remember feeling a special connection with an Italian girl, and being around her always brought positive vibes. However, when I shared my feelings with a few people, their negative comments stirred up some unwanted emotions in me.

I didn't realize it at the time, but I started drawing energy from sub-categories of hate because I was arbitrarily being denied the chance to fall in love. However, it wasn't about race; it was more about other people recognizing that she and I had feelings for each other, so they began using darker emotions to prevent real connections from forming. It worked, too, as I became more volatile, went missing in action, and eventually quit that job, ending up living out of my car. The only explanation I could find for these people's efforts to block a love connection is that our brains default against others' pursuit of positive feelings and our own.

When you think about people who draw energy from a dark source, you usually think of the villain in a story like *Star Wars*, such as Darth Vader. You don't consider the coworker or family member who comforts you in private but secretly tells others how sad and depressed you are. I had a close friend I confided in about my deepest secrets, only to realize one day that they betrayed me by sharing my confidential information with someone I despised. They didn't even apologize when I confronted them because they believed they were doing the right thing. All I can say is that I became the villain in that person's story and will stay in that role until I die. This further proves that we live in a universe meant to be chaotic and unbalanced. It's not supposed to be perfect because, if it were, there would be no hope or desire to seek the Light Realm.

Modern social media platforms reveal how subconscious minds often work against our conscious thoughts. Many successful content creators mention surrounding themselves with positive vibes because the comments section tends to be flooded with negativity. I doubt anyone would oppose a villain who aims to track IP addresses and harm those who make online negative comments anonymously. If we consider a killer who acts out of a comment, how much more would you admire this person if their actions completely eliminated negative comments because people now fear that such individuals will track their IP addresses? On the other hand, people can find others' IP addresses, which opens up many problems.

The Dark Realm skillfully influences people to tap into their negative emotional pools through their subtle thoughts. This is why we sometimes support the villain, because this dark energy can't grow without us. In fact, it's meant to grow, but if you root for the killer who kills someone we all hate, what emotional pool are we collectively pulling from? I guess the real question is whether we can all collectively have a positive emotion for an emotion in the negative pool without causing the dark energy force to grow?

The answer to the last question depends on whether your actions and those of others have attracted the attention of the Light Realm. You see, the Light Realm doesn't have to grow; it is a set entity with strict admission requirements, unlike the Dark Realm, which has a high acceptance rate. Pastor Joel Osteen shared that he never wanted to be a pastor of a megachurch because he was content working in the editor's room. Being on stage and in front of an audience makes him extremely uncomfortable, as it would any normal person. He didn't realize that his editing skills would help improve his voice's cadence. Because he spent years honing this skill indirectly, he never expected it would help draw millions toward believing in the Light Realm, including me. But these actions tend to compel the Light Realm to send particles your way. It's not about how many people you reach, but the positive feeling you give them that gains the attention of the Light Realm.

When I was in high school, I considered dropping out to sell drugs. Even though I watched my stepfather struggle with this, hard times put your thoughts in dark places and produce dark solutions. But if it weren't for a drug dealer threatening to harm me if he saw me on the streets, I wouldn't have earned three degrees today. Would you agree that the drug dealer was drawing positive emotions that could eventually lead him to the Light realm? What about the exotic dancer who doesn't drink, smoke, take men home, loves animals, and enjoys dancing for lonely men? Are they going to make it to the Light Realm?

Judgement Day

At one point, I was drawn to the Islamic faith because I admired how modest the women were. I believe women should be able to wear whatever they choose, but the ability to scroll through and gaze at the bodies of modern women has created a new kind of competition. Looking back, I remember many women in the early 2000s were slimmer, yet they were just as attractive due to their attitude.

These days, if you're looking for that cheerful attitude from a woman, it might come with a cost, but that's a story for another time. I thought that embracing the Islamic faith would help me steer clear of all that, but I've come to realize that a woman's attractiveness is closely tied to her virtues. Whether she's dressed modestly or in a more revealing way, deep down, she knows what kind of attraction she embodies. I experienced this firsthand when I tried to connect with the brothers at the local mosque. Everything was going smoothly until I noticed this stunning Arabian girl who also saw me—you can imagine, that's when my so-called brothers' competitive energy kicked in.

Living in the Hood was akin to being in a cauldron of unmanaged emotions. Many brothers I knew were cool before they got into gangs and trouble, but they didn't have the kind of beef with each other that could lead to violence until a girl got involved. It's worth discussing how a woman, like any other human, can evoke such strong emotional reactions in men, and how men can manage their emotions when a woman is involved.

I'm not going to give you a step-by-step guide because it's almost impossible to follow when you're just blocked and a few days later, you find out she's posting with a pretty boy from another part of town. Pretty Boy is definitely your Opp now, and since he's already from the other side, it's likely you'll feel tempted to jump into that negative vibe whenever you bump into him. The best thing you can do is acknowledge your feelings, which might feel like a strong red color, and imagine it as a gel or ball being gently lifted out of you. Remember, it's okay to feel this way—what matters most is how you handle those feelings as these negative particles from the dark energy force try to take over.

When one of the brothers at the mosque noticed me noticing her, all that brotherly energy shifted. I was new there, so I didn't feel comfortable asking who she was. I also noticed another girl of African background, and this guy, along with a few others, encouraged me to ask her out. We went out and had a good time, but there wasn't that strong romantic connection, enough to motivate me to perform my best every day. Everyone needs a healthy sexual relationship to feel their best, and if that's missing, it's natural to feel driven to find it. The brothers seemed sincere about supporting me, but I sensed some pressure to continue dating the African girl because I was Black, and they all thought it was a good match. The fact is, it wasn't a good match, and she and I knew it, just like the Arabian girl knew what she knew. To avoid any conflicts, I decided not to attend the service there anymore.

Part of me has always wondered what happened to that guy and the Arabian girl, but I knew it would be a mistake to let my emotions dwell on it, so I mentally moved on. My plan was to join the mosque, find a modest woman I was attracted to, and continue serving with my faith community. Good intentions, right? Years later, I tried the same approach at a church, and the same thing happened—this time with an American girl who admitted she sometimes did exotic dancing in a town a few hours away to make ends meet when things got tough. I couldn't understand how I had committed my actions both publicly and privately, only to not at least get my basic needs met. I started thinking about couples who lived righteously like I did and wanted a child, only to see them born with a disability, cancer, or some deformity, causing them to cry themselves to sleep every night because they feel shortchanged by the Divine.

Growing up in challenging environments influences the type of women one can attract, which can be either beneficial or detrimental. The true 'Gangster' derives satisfaction from engaging in mischievous activities, while others attempt to project toughness to deter such individuals from targeting them. Whether consciously acknowledged or not, these individuals are often considered the most resilient, earning respect from men and attraction from women. This resilience can be likened to social media popularity, where women aspire to be influential figures with numerous followers, whereas many other men are seen as average. Although this does not apply universally to all women, it is evident that physical fitness attracts attention. It is important to focus on the emotional awareness behind this attention, as a person perceived as a 'Gangster' might be deemed morally degenerate by a more refined individual who has graduated from a formal education college.

I never wanted to go to college. High school was tough enough, but getting good grades and dealing with people's judgment was the hardest part. I spent the first two years of high school hanging out with gang members and drug dealers, and ditching class because I didn't have suitable clothes. When I got a job at the local gas station, my grades improved because I had better clothes. It made me wonder why public schools don't have uniforms like private schools. Better yet, why not have gender-segregated classes for math and science so kids can concentrate more? At 16, I started thinking it was all a ploy to keep the class system in place. In my mind, this life was working for some college kid out there who just got into an Ivy League school and would one day own a company I was working for at the minimum wage rate. By 17, real anger about the life I was given began to grow in me.

Plus, I wasn't even attending my dream high school—West High on the other side of town. Deep down, I saw myself as someone from the Westside, and it just felt right that someone like me would go there. That made my first two years pretty tough. Things got better once I got a job and started hanging out with better friends. Still, I often have vivid dreams about going to West High School. These dreams feel so real that I've even started to think this version of me lives in another universe. I also dream about a different version of myself—one who didn't join the military or go to college, and who has two kids from two different women. This other version struggles to find work, and our mom keeps reminding me to take care of my kids while I still live with her. Sounds like a nightmare, doesn't it?

Fortunately, I joined the military and afterward attended a college in my hometown that I never thought I'd be able to attend. That's incredible, but how did I manage to finish college when I never wanted to go in the first place? It's simple: when you deliberately choose to draw from the Light Realm with positive feelings, it's like the Universe begins automatically guiding your path through your subconscious. I joined the military during the middle of the Iraq/Afghanistan War. Still, because I consciously decided not to lie to the Military Entrance Processing Station (MEPS) administrators, I was assigned to a duty station that let me attend college at night.

Anyone who's been through the MEPS process knows that right before they accept you, they do a thorough interview where you need to be completely honest and share everything before they perform the background check. So, I felt compelled to say I tried marijuana once when I was fourteen. My recruiter scolded me about this because he didn't understand why I needed to tell them something the background check wasn't capable of discovering, but what he or I didn't understand was that the Truth is a lifeform, among others, working for the Light Realm that helps navigate the judgment of your subconscious.

The Truth Shall Set You Free

Have you ever told a little white lie? Maybe someone asked how your weekend was, and you said you had the best time ever when you actually just relaxed and scrolled through social media. I remember being in San Diego, meeting three lovely girls, and even dancing with them—I never got their phone numbers, though. The next day, my friend asked what I did, and I shared what happened. When he asked if I got their contact info, I realized the truth was revealing itself. Should I have lied to make myself look better, or was it better to be honest? When I told him the truth, he just laughed because he already knew what it was. He understood the situation, and he just wanted to see if I'd be honest about it, matching what he was feeling inside. From that story at MEPS and what my friend wanted to check, I've learned that how you feel often matters more than the words you use when it comes to the truth. So, why do people sometimes choose to lie?

I'm sure some people have never told a lie in their lives, but if we made a movie about this person's story, it would flop because nobody would believe it. That's like asking a 25-year-old man if he's ever watched adult movies. Unless he doesn't have internet access, he's probably seen one or two. Since people can physiologically pick up on your actions, they can tell when you're lying, and that shouldn't go unnoticed. But what is a lie? If you feel deep down that you're meant to be a doctor who saves lives someday, is that actually a lie based on how you feel? What about the man who feels like a woman or a woman who thinks like a man? Even more, what about the black guy who sounds and acts like a white guy but doesn't have the skin tone to match? I don't have the answers to these questions, but I know it's an uphill battle with society's perception of who you are.

People often follow society's opinions and norms, choosing to support, oppose, or remain neutral about them. Usually, these ideas tell us what kind of thinking we should have, but luckily, they can't prevent us from growing. If someone is born with a leg deformity, becoming an Olympic track star might seem unlikely, but if your desire is truly strong, your chances of reaching that goal are high. The main thing is passion. Growing up in a low-income area, others might not expect you to achieve greatness, but when it happens, it feels like discovering gold in a land that's already struggling. For me, the biggest challenge was dealing with negative energy from the people around me. I remember finishing college and hearing a relative boast about earning a lot of money without going to school.

Be careful—anyone who tries to compete with you in a negative way can cause serious rifts in your subconscious routes.

When someone sees you as competition, they will never directly say that, but will use non-verbal cues to let you know. So, here is what you need to look for:

Are any of their mannerisms condescending?

Are you feeling awkward while talking to them?

Are they asking questions to get to know you, or does it feel like an investigation?

When you start asking them questions, do they answer completely?

Are they searching for weak points?

Are they vulnerable?

Do they want you to be vulnerable?

How long have you known them?

Some people are wonderful when you connect with them one-on-one, but things can change when you're in a larger group. Sometimes, they might share sensitive details about you intentionally, which can make you feel underestimated or less valued compared to others. This might be a way to keep everyone in line, and it can also be a reminder to appreciate the sense of belonging rather than feeling lonely. It can create an unspoken hierarchy that you're not even aware of. Being part of a group is fantastic, but remember, if you're invited, it might take some time to earn your place and for others to see your true worth. If they can't handle your independence and your ability to make your own choices, walking away might be the best option before any conflicts arise with the group's leader. Remember, some level of competitive energy is natural and healthy, but it's equally important to know when to step back and take a breather.

Having mental toughness means being confident and self-assured, knowing you can overcome any obstacle because you understand your abilities. This is just the basics, and it's tough for groups to get along with people like this, especially since they're self-motivated. I've learned that when it comes to competitive energy in groups, it's essential to keep conversations with each person positive. You should only open up when someone else does, and even then, you need to be cautious and willing to walk away if things get rocky. Genuine friendships take time to form and are just as challenging to maintain. I've been friends with five people for over a decade because we focus on staying positive and respecting boundaries.

I lost a good friend because he crossed the line with one comment about my baldness. It wasn't what he said; it was how he said it and the other conversations that led up to it. His tone changed once he realized he had presumably made more money than me. I let it go the first few times, but after the third time and the bald comment, I ended it and never spoke to him again. If someone indirectly disrespects you with their tone in front of your face, you can bet this person would humiliate you within a group. Before walking away, I recommend intentionally disrespecting them right off the bat until you guys are within the friend group to end the so-called friendship properly. Walking away quietly will only make you draw from negative emotions, so although this action seems to be drawing from dark energy, it's not based on the primary law of the Universe: what goes around comes right back around.

In the universe, you can't start a fight and expect to win it, but you'll always win what you didn't start. Mentally tough people usually achieve their goals because they know how to direct their subconscious thoughts toward their conscious goals; the gray area is when you put yourself on autopilot. Autopilot in the Thought Realm either leads to the Dark Realm or the Light Realm. For example, if you're always subconsciously directing your thoughts toward jealous behaviors, eventually you'll lose the ability to switch to the Light Realm. You can sense this negative energy from someone when they walk into the room. I remember always saying hello to a janitor, and he never said hello back. I never considered it rejection since I was focused on positive emotions. Several months later, I was told this gentleman died of a brain aneurysm, and they also shared that he was secretly in a hate group.

Like many others, this individual depended on the Dark Realm before physically entering it, as dark energy took over his thoughts, putting him on autopilot. When someone is on autopilot, their destination is mostly decided, which can be either helpful or harmful, depending on the mix of positive and negative emotions they've experienced in life. Every energy fuel vessel in the Universe has an equal chance—50/50—of heading to the Light or Dark Realm, ultimately based on their choice. If you think someone is being competitive with you but then find out they're competitive with several others, that person might be at risk of being led to the Dark Realm on autopilot. The collective consciousness, formed through group thoughts within the Thought Realm, plays a key role in determining autopilot. This isn't about specific individuals disliking you, but rather the energy you send out when interacting with others.

Have you ever heard wonderful things about someone before you met them, only to find that when you actually meet, the vibe feels a bit off? You know they're a good person, but for some reason, it doesn't seem like they genuinely like you, or maybe they even rub

80

you the wrong way. Since reaching the Light Realm can be a challenge, the Universe has created a balance of chaos — an ecosystem of emotions. A great way to see this is in a television series: in the first season, the two main characters are best friends, but by season two, they're bitter enemies, only to mend their relationship again in season three. Remember, our personality is never fixed; it's a fluid reflection of our experiences, setbacks, relationships, and growth. Our current personality essentially shows where we are in the Thought Realm. Keep in mind, as I mentioned earlier, we live in the Dark Realm because of the chaos, but that doesn't mean the dark energy totally consumes our thoughts; it just means we all aren't supposed to get along.

CHAPTER 5: THOUGHT LANES AND THE COLLECTIVE CONSCIOUSNESS

By limiting emotions to 27, the Universe makes it easier to distinguish right from wrong. As you review the list I provided earlier, you'll notice that negative feelings are nearly equally balanced with positive ones. To figure out whether you're tapping into the dark or Light Realm, constantly check this list and pay attention to which ones trigger the strongest physical responses. Here's the list again:

- Admiration

- Adoration

- Aesthetic appreciation

- Amusement

- Anxiety

- Awe

- Awkwardness

- Boredom

- Calmness

- Confusion

- Craving

- Disgust

- Empathetic pain

- Entrancement

- Envy

- Excitement

- Fear

- Horror

- Interest

- Joy

- Nostalgia

- Romance

- Sadness

- Satisfaction

- Sexual desire

- Sympathy

- Triumph

As I wrote this book, three emotions stood out to me: Satisfaction, Aesthetic Appreciation, and Triumph. Do you agree that these are all positive emotions? Here's the key: think of this list as a menu rather than a system that automatically chooses for you. I once knew a guy everyone spoke highly of, but I knew he didn't like me when we met because I could feel it. I remember him making a comment about light-skinned Black people, but I didn't pay much attention to it until we started having problems. Even though there are over a hundred skin tones worldwide, colorism has fueled some of the strongest negative emotions known to humankind. I'm not sure when the skin-tone epidemic began, but the skin-tone relationship has been the main factor in deciding which Thought realm lane you're in.

If you ask someone if emeralds are better than rocks, they'd need to see a rock first, not be color blind, and, of course, have eyes to see. If that person was blind and you told them to choose which is better, they'd have to feel it out. Once someone tells the blind person he chose the wrong one, he might feel envy toward the one with eyes or accept life as he knows it. On the other hand, if the person with eyes is told he's color blind, they could go either way when choosing which Thought Realm to be in. The word "could" here is conditional because that's the choice the Universe has imposed on you to restrict access to the Light Realm.

I considered different factors when I shared my emotions. The second one, Aesthetic Appreciation, was because I've lost weight and have a limited income. Thinking about craving food while broke triggers Fear, which comes from dark energy. I chose Satisfaction first because I want to spend my day writing something meaningful, and I look forward to Triumph when I finish this book. I viewed my Menu of Emotions and consciously engaged all three to steer my thoughts toward the Light Realm, putting myself in that thought lane. Your choices in thought connect you to the Collective Consciousness, which is why you keep meeting the same person.

I live in an apartment with over two hundred others, but I always see the same people. Are all the other residents avoiding contact and never stepping outside? Not at all! Because the collective consciousness exists around us, it functions like a highway, keeping all emotions in motion. Like any road, lane, or expressway, your life can experience delays, roadblocks, heavy traffic, aggressive drivers, and accidents. However, the emotion you select from the menu will guide new paths of experiences with drivers who share similar feelings and choices. Many religious organizations suggest that if you mess up in the eyes of God, you'll face more hardships. I'd say that even if you live a perfect, godly life, hardships are inevitable because we exist in a realm of conflict. So why are there tests and hardships?

Imagine growing up in Utah in a peaceful environment free from cursing, secular music and movies, with well-kept lawns, no tattoos, and fresh-smelling air. You go to school and meet the love of your life while attending college. You get married and have three wonderful kids. As your children grow, you teach them right from wrong based on one of your religious guides, and they seem happy, which makes you happy too. Everything is perfect until a tragedy occurs: your oldest child dies in a car crash while hanging out with friends. A few years later, your youngest daughter becomes a tyrant because she prefers girls over boys, and you can't accept that because of how you were raised. For many years, you try to change her, but she resists every attempt. Eventually, she moves to California to create adult content, which devastates your core emotions. You wonder if you did something wrong—what could it have been?

Although your middle child grew up well, your overwhelming emotions are focused on your youngest child because you believe that dark energy somehow took control of her mind. You think her influence came from a song or a movie that affected her. As a result, she becomes a well-known adult star whom you condemn and stop speaking to after she has already left your life, expecting to hear that she's possibly dead in a hotel. However, after 15 years, she is still in the adult film industry but has a family and children. Seeing that your middle child and his wife couldn't have biological kids, your daughter's children are your only biological grandchildren. You want a relationship with them as you grow older, so you reach out to your adult film star daughter for the first time in 20 years.

Even though she is resistant, your daughter wants to discuss the pain you caused her, and you go along because you need a relationship with your grandchildren. You argue that it was the music that made her bisexual and led her to her adult career, but she claims she was always attracted to women as a child and was proud to be an adult film star who made others feel good. You can't handle the blasphemy, so you end the conversation just like before. Years later, one of her kids, your grandson, gets accepted to the same college you attended in Utah and wants to visit you on weekends. During these visits, your grandson tells you that, despite his mother or your daughter being in the adult industry, they had a great childhood with close friends and a loving household. You feel so guilty that you decide to visit your daughter in California, who is now retired from the industry.

On your way there to hopefully mend things, you have a heart attack. While you recover, you hope your daughter visits you, but she never does. Your grandson and his fiancée come and show you a video of an interview she did about the pain she felt growing up, knowing she felt being bisexual was natural to who she was, even though she fell in love with a man and had a wonderful family with him. That night, you die, still confused because your daughter's actions and life were against everything your religious guide taught you to be correct and acceptable to gain access to Heaven. Whose life was in the wrong here?

The story I just shared with you is the only true reality of life on earth, while every other perfect story with flawless scenarios leading to perfect outcomes only exists in the Light Realm. Don't misunderstand; you will experience normality, like traveling to work or school every day and reaching your destination without issues, but remember that the road knows what we do not. Your job is to guide your thoughts, which come from choosing from the Menu of Emotions. Before I started writing, I struggled with a lot of depression, and my dad didn't understand why, so he blamed my mom for dropping me as a baby because he equated this to my mental neurosis. As a young kid, I always knew I was different, noticing that I didn't want to hang out in groups and preferred to be alone to read. When I got older, my dad felt like a woman, and kids would keep me out of a depressed state of mind, but he never knew that writing books and movies truly made me happy. If I hadn't been depressed, I would have never found my most genuine passions in life that made me feel fulfilled.

The Adult Content Creator felt a deep sense of joy because she was helping couples enjoy a healthy and happy sex life through her videos. Sadly, her parents passed away, feeling confused. According to the laws of Collective Consciousness, when you consistently pull out and evoke positive emotions from the Menu of Emotions throughout your life, your existence naturally tends to gravitate toward the Light Realm. Moreover, the Collective Consciousness wonderfully gauges these emotions through the people you meet and connect with every day.

Adult content creators and stars are part of our emotional ecosystem, but if someone becomes too reliant on this content, it can harm their ability to handle real-life situations, making it tougher to form meaningful emotional bonds. Some people claim that adult content overall kills romance, but isn't sexual attraction crucial to falling in love? The next chapter will explore this idea further.

What You Need For Love

I won't lie and say I don't watch adult content because I do, just not very often. When I do, I usually focus on the same performer, if you get what I mean. Is this hurting my chances at love? I've noticed that when I watch any type of adult content, strange people tend to come into my path, but that's only because I sometimes feel negative emotions afterward; that's just my experience, though it might be different for others. Since I've felt real love connections before, I know they're different from infatuation or sexual desire, so I'd say no. These strange people appearing around me are something to pay attention to. Sexual desire is an emotion that can sometimes lead you into the depths of the Dark Realm, unfortunately, and dark energy has taken hold of many because of this. So, let me share the best guidance I can on how to handle this.

Men, a woman's heart is connected to her clitoris, meaning her heart rate needs to synchronize with yours in the same environment before she genuinely feels attracted to you. The only way to sync with her heart rate is to establish an emotional connection. If you can't make this connection, you risk getting rejected or, worse, being played, since she knows you only want her physically, not emotionally. Measuring the net effect of adult content and drug use during initial exposure can create powerful positive emotions throughout your mind and body. However, because negative emotions often have a stronger impact afterwards, you may be drawn to dark energy forces autopilot mode.

When someone autopilots toward the dark energy source, they become indifferent to emotions that could bring them closer to the Light Realm. Thinking of Anakin Skywalker from the *Star Wars* movies, he was a good man until fear took over his mind. His love interest, Padmé, tried to save him with her love, but it was too late because his mind was consumed by dark energy, which caused his destructive actions against the universe. Think about yourself now as you wake up in an emotional state. Would you say you're like that all day? I remember a time when I woke up every day feeling depressed, so I blamed God, which led to anger. I became angry at anyone I believed had it better than me, so as a black man, I targeted white people. You see, when I was growing up in the hood, I never thought about it, but once I learned that many whites built societal structures to keep themselves in a superior position, it truly angered me.

This anger triggered a lot of hostility among many white people, at least in my energy field; it was as if they could sense the dark energy particles influencing me. Because I was allowing anger to take over, many other negative emotions grew stronger. I believe this was the dark energy force-feeding me; more so, it could put me on autopilot. Ironically, my sexual desire for white women increased dramatically during this period, and I noticed myself around more bigots because of the Thought Lane I was in. I honestly believe my sexual desire rose because the Light Energy was responding strongly to try to prevent me from being completely taken over. It was a powerful attempt to save me from entering Autopilot. Even with this, the Autopilot toward the Light Realm does not try to pull everyone in because of its restrictive measures, so you must make the right emotional and conscious choices.

Have you ever gone to school with a troublemaker, and someone's trying to save them even though everyone knows they're headed nowhere? I was once seen as a troublemaker, but I never believed I wouldn't make something of my life. I was definitely angry about the life I was given, but I always held onto hope that I would become something. Growing up in a tough neighborhood can make it hard to find a genuine smile, but since you're at the bottom, you have something to aim for—the purest form of hope. I grew up on a hill with mostly Black residents, so issues like racism and bigotry weren't a big factor. What was a factor was getting bullied because I didn't have nice clothes and shoes. The only others I thought who had it worse than us were the white family who lived down the hill, who had a kid my age. Let me tell you a story about Jackson.

Jackson, a pseudonym, was a low-income white boy who was bullied because others thought he was too intelligent and outspoken. Although he was bigger and not targeted physically, he often used big words to belittle others, especially Black kids. One day during lunch, they all decided to attack him by kicking and throwing rocks. Jackson ended up bruised, bloodied, and crying, which led to his removal from school. I don't know if I participated in the assault in this fictional story, but with about ten kids involved, I felt partly responsible, especially since I didn't help him. I didn't see Jackson again until our senior year, when he had become a full-blown bigot.

Jackson hated blacks and refused to talk to any of us. I had Jackson in my Study Hall with another guy who was on edge with blacks, but wasn't quite as extreme as Jackson; we'll give this guy the fictitious name of Pete. In the Study Hall, Pete and I would always discuss race and what he thought blacks should do to better themselves, or, better yet, be more like whites in terms of social, economic, and educational values. Many of his points were valid, so I could only agree, and because of this, Pete and Jackson gave me a pass. Although I was given a pass, Jackson straight-up let me know he didn't like blacks, but I never pressed him on this issue because I knew where it was rooted.

After I joined the military, I found out Jackson had killed a relative of mine. I used to hang out with this relative as a kid, but I hadn't seen him in 10 years. Not only did Jackson kill my relative, but he and his girlfriend dismembered the body, then proceeded to have intercourse with the dead bodies still in the room. When the police arrived, they stated it was a party atmosphere that so happened to have a couple of dead bodies.

A few years after this happened, I watched some interviews of Jackson after he received a life sentence, and he seemed happy about his life, as if he had no remorse for what he did. You see, Jackson wanted to kill a black person because the dark energy would stop at nothing to have his thoughts, so once those dark particles had complete control, he was on autopilot. I recently looked up Jackson and found photos and stories about him, in which he seemed to have lost every ounce of positive emotional particles one could imagine. Because of Jackson, I now know how one can forever lose the positive emotions needed for love and ultimately access to the Light Realm.

Black Hate

Jackson allowed his hatred for blacks to hinder his ability to make positive contributions to others' lives. As I mentioned earlier, I began reflecting on this same thought process when I went to college, but I recognized the dangerous path it could lead me down. I've always been respected for demonstrating my work skills, but to develop those skills, I first needed motivation, which didn't come easily. As the Earth reaches its capacity to support life, natural and artificial calamities will occur to maintain the planet's ecological balance. Competition for resources will intensify, along with tensions among humans. However, this tension has been a part of all communities worldwide for a long time, so what's the real issue?

Leading Black conservative economists share their insights on why Black men may sometimes face challenges in economic growth, while also appreciating the numerous opportunities America has offered. I genuinely respect economists like Thomas

Sowell, though I see them as far from being comparable to the shadowy tactics of dark energy forces.

Mr. Sowell grew up in a New York ghetto, joined the military, then got into Harvard, and now earns a living as a writer who contributes to the collective consciousness of the intelligentsia. Because he's one of the most intellectually gifted Black men of the past two centuries, his words carry significantly more weight than Tyrone from the Hood, who also has the same level of IQ but speaks with a dialect most suburban and rural whites find hard to hear. Tyrone can't articulate himself properly, so he can't get a job, and since obtaining a job or a business loan is unlikely, he becomes one of the 3 out of 4 Black men statistics Mr. Sowell and others are paid well to criticize, thus fueling ongoing tactics that create division and chaos.

While growing up in the Hood, I've seen some brilliant guys give up on the American dream because of the tactics used by the competitive social infrastructure. Don't get it wrong; this infrastructure isn't exclusive to whites but is a more adaptable preconceived skillset shaped by the collective consciousness. I'm not suggesting that these preconceived skills are tied to cultural differences; I'm mainly highlighting the intense critique within and outside a person's perceived culture. For example, a Black American doctor with a few tattoos and an urban dialect will feel the pressure from both within and outside his perceived culture, as his Thought Lane can't be clearly identified. The chances of him progressing through his culture to become a doctor of any kind are about 1 in 100, given the cultural pressures. So, how does one manage to do it?

Back in the 1950s, many families shaped their family structures in hopes of paving the way for their children's success. The Civil Rights Act of 1964 aimed to promote integration, but it unintentionally widened social and economic gaps because of resistance rooted in the imbalance between the Dark and Light Realms. For instance, although the government wanted to integrate schools, many white families chose to send their children to private schools because Black students often scored lower on standardized tests.

When I first discovered this, I felt angry because it seemed like Black people were less intelligent. However, as I looked deeper, I began to understand the broader context of whites wanting their children to stay on course. Still, that didn't completely dispel my anger, especially since many white people subconsciously show signs of these social and economic divisions—particularly when you don't look or sound like them. What I found was that it's not a white or Black issue; it's a strategy of the dark energy force to find ways to be completely absorbed by its particles.

So, how does this dark energy create the feeling of division? It does so by making people see themselves as either better or worse than others, often based on things like race or education. As I mentioned earlier, my white friend from high school study hall wanted Blacks to be more like whites, and because I agreed with some of his points, we became friends. But what if I hadn't had the insight to do that? It's possible we might have had conflicts, and Pete might have even hurt me and been in jail with his friend Jackson for a hate crime. Luckily, that story never came to be because Pete and I were able to find a way to share a positive emotion, which caught the attention of the Light Realm and helped guide us onto better paths.

When I think about entire groups of people doing something that captures the Light Energy Realms' attention, I think of globalization. I'm not a professor, nor is this a business class, but for example, white Americans have collectively developed innovative business processes that have improved the world. Today, many races contribute to global commerce, but whites are not the primary experts in creating dance, food, and being culturally trendy. We can acknowledge achievements where they're due, but we all contribute collectively in our own way.

Thought Lanes

I've mentioned thought lanes before, but now I'll explain them in more detail. Stereotypes arise from group generalizations, and these thought lanes are the mental pathways that we and others create to categorize us before our true appeal. Essentially, thought lanes are marketplaces of ideas that we borrow from to boost our cognitive abilities. Usually, these lanes are populated by individuals sharing the same cultural background, which here refers more to inherited culture than personal identity. For example, your conscious mind might think it's reasonable to trust black experts in basketball and rap because we witness their expertise firsthand, rather than it being just a stereotype. Nonetheless, desire often overrides the generalizations held by the stewards of these thought lanes.

I once aspired to be a basketball player because I was tall, not due to race. Reflecting on this dream, I also think of the community that encouraged me, helping me feel positive emotions about this goal that I believed I could achieve as a young man. These individuals believed in my potential, not out of generalizations but because they genuinely wanted to see me succeed. If I were shorter, I doubt I would have considered a career in basketball unless I truly wanted it internally. This highlights the difference between internal and external desires and reflects the greatness of truly skilled individuals. When you commit to a path, critics may challenge you, but if your desire is genuine, you often inspire others along the way.

I never thought about becoming a writer before, during, or even right after college- yet you're reading this. Where did my desire to write originate? In high school, I did okay but excelled in English; I don't know why, but I just did. They say that human DNA is 99.6 percent the same across everyone, but that tiny .4 percent gives us our unique identity. My mother's .4 percent had a distinct imprint as a writer. Sadly, she wasn't encouraged to pursue that passion because her mother wanted her to play with other kids instead of being alone in a room, jotting down her thoughts. You see, my mother had an internal desire to be a writer but lacked external support. Malcolm X comes to mind regarding internal versus external influences; he internally wanted to be a lawyer, but was discouraged at a young age because his grade school teacher saw different success paths for black students at that time.

The Universe will interpret your idea of success by assessing your daily emotional states and how you harness these emotions to achieve your broader conscious goals. It is well understood that the universe is expanding; however, this suggests that the surrounding energy will naturally seek its evolution. Can you imagine a world where humans are as large as planets, or where worlds exist within worlds smaller than an atom? Although these ideas are purely imaginative, it is this very imagination that fuels dreams becoming reality. The most valuable resource is information, and as the human brain emits information, a concern arises when people allow anger or hatred to dominate their subconscious thoughts. This indicates that humanity is falling further behind in its evolutionary journey. Why do we keep depicting flying cars in movies rather than making them real? The answer is that we spend more time sedating that .4 percent rather than putting energy into nurturing its growth.

Imagine a man who has lived forty years on Earth with no significant mark, graduated from high school, had a couple of kids, and now works a blue-collar manufacturing job in the Midwest. After ten years, he has identified a few product process improvements but is too scared to speak up, so another five years go by without him saying a word. When the company's products start declining in the market, it lays off everyone and files for bankruptcy. He finds another job and spends the rest of his life raising his kids and grandchildren, who follow the same path. This analogy represents the subconscious behavior pattern that the other 99.6 percent thrive on daily, which numbs them from what society's dreamers truly envision at night. As a kid, you're taught to dream, but by age 30, many fall under the pressure of starting a family and holding down a regular job to support themselves. Being a dreamer at this stage becomes risky, especially when bills are piling up, and any abstract ideas you want to pursue become null and void.

Remember when I mentioned how my mom dreamed of being a writer but faced some discouragement? After having four children, she decided to try her hand at singing, entering local talent shows, even though it didn't lead to big success. I remember the day she decided to stop—she had an audition at a local school. I was outside the hallway with my brother, feeling so proud and excited for her, but when she came out, she was overwhelmed with emotion and didn't perform. I also have a relative who was quite similar. He showcased his talent at various shows around the Chicagoland area, but things didn't really take off when he moved to Atlanta. They didn't know it at the time, but both of them inspired me to chase my dreams of writing with determination, no matter the obstacles. More than that, they helped me see where I might face setbacks. One of the first people I met after moving to California was a woman with kids who writes songs and demos for major artists. Thinking of my mom and cousin, I realized that setbacks can be part of the journey, and they pushed me to keep going.

You don't own your ideas; the Universe owns every idea and connected experience. This same Universe can also regulate time, but it doesn't own it—only the Light and Dark Realms control our time-experience milestones, and they're not shared equally. As I mentioned, our thoughts tend to drift toward dark energy because we live in the Dark Realm. Although challenging, consider that just as water seeks its own level through the water cycle, you should see yourself living within this realm in a similar way. Despite its chaos, the water cycle is driven by the sun. Some might argue that the Light

Realm exists within the sun because, without the sun generating energy for the water cycle here on Earth, we would perish. The water cycle's existence is proof of an all-powerful energy source—something humans can't create or control, but merely observe as an Absolute. Why not choose to flow toward something that is a source for all living things, an energy of motion that even darkness cannot stop?

Whenever I find myself drifting into negative thoughts or emotions, I turn to the oceans or any moving water to guide me back to the light. I remember the first time I read about how Black people were enslaved in this country, then the Jim Crow era, and later, racism in business during the 90s, and I felt overwhelming anger toward white Americans. Additionally, the Universe kept placing me among extremely bigoted people to add fuel to that fire.

I was very close to committing a crime due to the constant anger I was feeling, but when I received my orders to San Diego, it shifted my mindset. Don't get it wrong, California isn't any different in terms of harnessing racial tension, but the energy near the ocean eased me. I don't know where you are, but at this point, you're about seventy percent through this book, so I suggest you take an extended break from reading this, find a large body of moving water, and sit quietly to think about what gives you life as you know it. Once you return, the rest of this book will help you draw from positive emotions.

CHAPTER 6: PULLING FROM WITHIN

I want to categorize the 27 distinct emotions identified by the University of Berkeley into negative and positive groups to help you better understand their connection to your Thought Lanes and experiences. Below is the list for both categories.

Positive	**Negative**
Admiration	Anger
Adoration	Anxiety
Aesthetic Appreciation	Awkwardness
Amusement	Boredom
Awe	Confusion
Calmness	Craving
Empathic Pain	Disgust
Excitement	Entrancement
Interest	Fear
Joy	Horror

Nostalgia   Sadness

Relief   Sexual Desire

Romance

Satisfaction

Surprise

As you can see, the positive outweighs the negative by a factor of three. I'll share my own story with each one, but I encourage you to think about the word, then the first emotion that comes to mind, followed by a memory or experience associated with that word.

We'll start with the negative pool first to clear all the cobwebs before we end the book with the good stuff.

Chapter 7: Emotions

Anxiety

When I reflect on this word, the first image that comes to mind is a car speeding past me and everyone else on the road, trying to cause an accident because they didn't wake up on time for work. I also feel the nerves shooting through my body as I constantly check my rearview mirror, hoping no one is tailgating me to get to work. Honestly, I never understood what anxiety truly was until I started going to therapy, but now I realize it's a need for personal space, no matter where you are. Sometimes, I think about living off the grid, but I still need social interaction and, honestly, for others to give me some space. Anxiety is this uneasy feeling that often pops up when you're in a place or around people who throw you off balance. Let's start by exploring the aspect of location.

A town I once lived in had three gyms that interested me: one in the east, one in the west, and another northeast of my home. Since the west gym wasn't built yet, I visited the eastern one first. Every visit made me feel uncomfortable with the staff and members, and even the equipment's arrangement disrupted my energy. Despite this, I continued because it was closest to my house. After ten visits, I realized I could visualize my feelings of worry, irritation, and a sense of danger as if it was an orange, gel-like ball floating in front of me. I asked myself, "Is this the mood I want to carry from this gym?" If the place's electromagnetic energy seems to reject me, I accept this feeling as a sign to leave and consider it a lesson learned. When invited somewhere by a friend, this feeling might be skewed—if that gel ball grows or nearly explodes, it's a cue to leave immediately!

I remember meeting this beautiful girl with a scar on her left cheek. She told me she got it during a fight at a bar on the side of town she rarely visits. When I asked her why she didn't leave if she felt unsafe, she said her friend was having a good time and didn't want to leave, even though she sensed danger from some random girls staring at her; one of those girls gave her that scar for life. She couldn't listen to her subconscious feelings because her conscious feelings wanted to stay with her friend. So, how does one deal with this common situation? People often say to listen to your gut or heart, but in this case, her risk of ending up with a lifelong scar was losing the friend who originally invited her there. Her friend should have recognized her feelings before going—either through words or non-verbal cues.

These feelings aren't just about places like the gym; they can also relate to cities, regions, states, or countries. My advice for anyone, place, or thing you have a chemical imbalance with is to reject it as much as it rejects you because the Universe is doing you a favor by giving you negative feelings, but this only applies if you're in the negative emotional pool. That's why it is crucial to focus on building positive energy so you can avoid lifelong scars.

Awkwardness

When was the last time you attended a gathering and truly felt welcomed, experiencing love from everyone there? Probably never, right? Usually, you try to figure out who will be there before deciding whether to go. I don't understand why people think they can avoid someone they have issues with at a party, only to arrive and see that very person snickering at them from the corner. Unless someone is neurodivergent, this kind of social behavior can trigger a fight-or-flight response, and most people choose to avoid conflict. Or, you could make the party a real hit by going over there and slapping the **** out of them; now that's a case of drawing from both emotional pools if you catch my drift.

Anyone who has attended school from adolescence to early 20s has encountered awkward situations. My first two years of high school were particularly uncomfortable. Since my mother supported us alone, she had to focus on paying bills instead of buying new school clothes. Because I didn't have proper school attire or had to wear the same outfit twice a week, I would check the school attendance policy and intentionally skip school on days I had nothing to wear. Avoiding these awkward moments might seem like missing out on important information for my future, but it was a choice between being teased, which could lead to fights and expulsion. The tradeoff was a low ACT score, which prevented me from attending top colleges, but by age 35, I had earned three degrees and worked on multimillion-dollar contracts with people from Harvard University.

Previously, I mentioned going after your Opps, and in the case of the snickering coworker in the corner, you can choose to confront this person or avoid the situation entirely by skipping the party. Do what you feel is best to reach the Light Realm. Some people need to confront the snickering because it's been going on for too long. Therefore, it must stop; for others, this person may end up reporting to you and eventually resigning, but it's important to listen to your feelings to determine the right course. If you can't avoid the awkwardness, take it as a learning experience for growth. I remember liking a girl and sending her a few messages, but she replied that I should leave her alone or that she would report me. Talk about awkward! Instead of continuing to ask her questions, I once again thought that someone else might be way better for me, so I needed to go out there and find her.

Better feelings exist in and around us, so there's no excuse to avoid the negative ones. To go back to my mom, she's always telling people about my college degrees instead of having to explain why her third son can't keep a job because he dropped out of high school for fighting. Like your feelings, positive and negative energy live in and around us, so we can make the best decisions. If you don't know, energy isn't limited by time, and I believe that a person's dreams can also steer your feelings in the right direction, but we will discuss that later. Thought paths to the Light Realm don't seem rewarding because they often don't produce immediate results, but the overall impact is so profound you wouldn't even imagine what you'll gain.

Although my energy might not match the vibe of places like Minnesota or Riverside, CA, I'm genuinely grateful for how they've helped me grow in ways I never expected. I'll keep sharing my thoughts about these places because they made me feel a bit awkward, but I truly understand that they bring wonderful feelings to others. It's a bit like seeing a happy couple in public when you're single: rather than feeling awkward, it's a perfect moment to reflect on what you will have someday. The Universe guides us to where we're meant to be, based on the positive thoughts we choose to focus on.

Boredom

This feeling is probably the main reason many turn to drugs and alcohol, so brace yourself for a long read—just kidding. But seriously, party drugs and alcohol draw out people's fun side, which explains why many enjoy them. I've gained a lot of courage from that bottle of gold, but looking back at the good times, I was never truly drunk—just a little more confident. That's the level I believe people should stay at, in my opinion. Even with marijuana, it seems people can tell from your aura whether you smoke, and they want to hang out with you based solely on that. My first experience with smoking was negative, especially since my mother portrayed it as a very evil habit during my upbringing, which made me associate it with dark energy. However, others may feel differently, and that's okay.

I'm not here to explore the topic of drugs and alcohol in depth. While the Bible mentions turning water into wine, it also warns against overindulgence. So, is it possible to enjoy drinks or smoking daily for that good vibe while still staying true to the Light Energy path? I believe it varies depending on how it feels for each person in their own moment. Some folks choose to avoid alcohol altogether, sometimes missing out on parties because others might see them as boring. When I first started going out, I wasn't a heavy drinker, but I noticed that going without a drink made everything feel a bit dull. On the flip side, I've been to religious gatherings where we'd hang out after services and have a fantastic time without any alcohol or drugs around. This makes me think about whether abstaining from substances helps us stay on a positive, harmonious frequency that aligns with the natural energy of religious groups.

Many people see religious groups and their events as dull and lacking energy, mainly because they focus on the afterlife. I remember talking with a deeply spiritual person about the Bible verse regarding turning water into wine. His answer focused on resisting the influence of evil spirits on his soul, similar to the effects of drinking alcohol, using drugs, and watching adult content. From a biological standpoint, I understand the negative effects of heavy drinking; however, socially, moderate drinking is usually accepted. If you believe evil spirits will bother you because of drinking, then by all means, avoid it! I also suggest being prepared for the fact that many people might choose not to socialize with you because you don't drink. It is commendable but socially difficult, and the same goes for smokers.

Life can't be exciting all the time, so during boring moments, you must understand that there's no excitement without boredom. I grew up during a time when being dull or boring meant prioritizing your intellect over appearance. Nobody earned cool points for getting straight A's in school; it was more about having the newest brand-name sneakers and the trendiest clothes to attract the most beautiful girl. Maybe things have changed since the early 2000s, but nothing is more boring than an ambitious guy spending his Saturday night working on his invention instead of going out drinking and partying with friends. On the flip side, when that same guy becomes wealthy from his invention, all the coolness is in full swing, making those boring times look like productive phases that lead to incredible moments. I actively try to turn my boring moments into productivity because I know this will lead to feelings of excitement beyond belief.

Confusion

When I consider confusion, I often think about gay individuals. Have you ever wondered how someone can be both gay and religious? Gay people often recognize their attractions early on, but conservative religions tend to see it differently. Humans have an innate tendency to assert what we believe is right or wrong, but this anomaly in human evolution must not be overlooked. I know many gay individuals, and as a straight man, I've always wondered why they aren't attracted to the opposite sex, especially from a spiritual angle. I knew two men in the military who confided in me that they were gay—both white, one from Boston and the other from Utah. This was during the era of "Don't Ask, Don't Tell," so I kept quiet. Looking back, I wonder why they felt so comfortable sharing with me and why I never reported them to leadership to have them discharged. A few years ago, I found the answer deep within myself.

The way questions about being gay were always answered involved the birds and the bees analogy. Biologically, I saw birds as symbols of wholeness, while bees signified a sting, and surprisingly, life would continue. Over time, I began to reflect on my own attractions and how others viewed them. I've known since my youth that I was attracted to a particular type of person, but I kept it a secret to preserve social harmony. As I got older, the desire for this specific type of person grew stronger, yet I continued to suppress it, as if placing heavy screwdrivers on a lid to keep it sealed. Every relationship I had conformed to this social order, but I felt the pressure mounting; my lie was slipping free from the truth. Eventually, this pressure erupted in the one place all humans share—the bedroom.

Stage fright in the bedroom clears up all confusion. You can't create sensual chemistry, especially if you try—each time I went out with someone I wasn't feeling the vibe with to fit into the 'social order,' it only deepened the confusion. As the misery set in, I began to understand why some people cheat. Keep in mind, my tendency to focus on negative feelings persisted, so choosing to date someone socially acceptable rather than someone I genuinely liked left me drawing from negative energy.

Who was this person? A more meaningful question might be who I truly am. I once asked my mentor who he thought I was most attracted to, and he said she would resemble singer and actress Jennifer Lopez. While public figures are just ideas, I made a list of everyone I felt an immediate attraction to when I met them in person. I also took time to reflect on my interactions with these individuals and how they engaged with me. The results surprised me! Out of the nine people I listed, all were women with a variety of skin tones. When I think about their personality traits, those also differed, but one thing they all shared was excelling at something, which seemed to be a common denominator.

As social media's influence grows, algorithms often steer us toward similar thoughts about our desires, suggesting that everyone wants the same thing. I prefer to step back from this trend, listen to my emotions, and then make decisions based on them. Our feelings mirror the truth of the collective consciousness that surrounds us. If you experience feelings that go against the mainstream but feel right to you, it might be a sign to make a significant change, or else negative energy could take over.

Craving

In today's world, relationships often feel like a struggle, regardless of the circumstances. As I mentioned earlier, I discussed how people tend to judge who is paired with whom, but does that really matter? Throughout my life, I've approached many women, which raises concerns about society's perceptions of what's deemed appropriate for me. However, my own preferences are entirely different. Before I describe the kind of person I find attractive, I want to share some background on my mother's dating history, as her experiences have shaped my thoughts and energy. My mother, born in Mississippi, had me as her third child with her third partner—all before she turned 22. She was unique, possessing both a gift and a curse; she had a body many men desired. As a child, I didn't think much of it because she was my mom, but once I reached adulthood, I realized that the institution of sex can trap you in the same thought patterns forever!

I've experienced chemistry with women of various types, often initially attracted to their physical traits, but a true connection only formed once subconscious thoughts linked us. For instance, my first two chemistry-filled encounters were with slim women who enjoyed reading, creating a deeper bond. The third woman I felt a vibe with possessed more commanding physical features and was purely sexual in my perception. She liked reading too, but her social media presence was stronger, as she was a visual artist. When she entered a room, she naturally drew attention due to her body, whereas the first two women often entered unnoticed and spent most of their time studying. Reflecting on my mother in comparison to these women, the third woman came to mind—she often attracted male attention but rarely read anything beyond the Bible. So, do women with more prominent physical features struggle more with intellectual pursuits, or has the Universe shortchanged them in that aspect?

Our minds often consider what-ifs. I believe that if my mom hadn't had her figure, she probably wouldn't have gotten pregnant at 14. She might have focused more on school instead of being distracted by attention from boys, which could have allowed her classmates to concentrate better as well. However, when I went to college and saw many women with similar attractive features who also prioritized academics, I questioned this idea. I called my mother to ask about her school experiences; she mostly described how boys fought over her, not her academic pursuits. Looking at her siblings, I realized most conversations centered around finding a partner and having children, which many of my cousins did early. This pattern had been passed down, trapping us all in the same Thought Lane.

I was determined to change my approach by focusing solely on academics and finding someone who shared similar interests. Instead of judging women by their appearance, I observed their academic pursuits. I approached them based on that, only asking for their contact information if I felt we were intellectually compatible. Many women will dislike what I'm about to say, but it didn't take long for me to realize that this approach was likely to fail. The main reason was that we didn't have strong enough sexual attraction to push through the difficult parts of a relationship. It's ideal to have a deep intellectual connection, but that connection also needs to translate to the physical aspect as well.

My mother ended up marrying my stepfather, whom we all disliked until his untimely death. Ironically, she never had children with him, but they shared unconditional love. Growing up, my stepfather was a drug dealer and, at some point, became addicted. Some positive things about him were that he was a hard worker, gave her money when needed, and never crossed any boundaries as our stepfather—he mostly stayed quiet and knew his place. Even with a few domestic issues caused by their love while we were kids, we all knew their love for each other was unbreakable because of the way my mom would feel when he came back around. Even though I despise this man, he had a purpose: to give loving energy to my mom so she could do her best to love us, and I thank him for that.

Men, or the person considered the man in a relationship, play a crucial role because their actions influence the emotional stability of the partnership. I recall my stepfather joking that he wanted my mom for her backside, while she loved his eyes. Although it might seem trivial, this perspective helped them generate positive energy, creating a strong foundation for their love. No woman wants to be viewed as a sex object unless she is a sex worker, but I believe the genuine chemistry between my mother and stepfather stemmed from their shared subconscious understanding. Ironically, my mother was strongly against drugs, including marijuana, as if it were the worst sin. She believed weed and crack were the same and passed this mentality to my brothers and me.

When I think about their relationship, she was his yin to his yang, meaning the counter to his addiction, which is why it lasted so long. I think we all crave a certain type of person, but will they offset your imbalance or more so lead you to the Light Realm? How do you feel about this person outside of the physical stuff? Like I mentioned before, I tend to go against the algorithm market trends so that I can go beyond my cravings to find the benefit of fasting for something that will make me stronger.

Disgust

I can interpret the word "disgust" in many ways, but what matters most is the feeling it evokes. When I think of this word, I recall a girl I met at a retail store who seemed pretty cool. However, once we started texting, I realized she had a different perspective than I did. This girl was lovely, and we had sexual chemistry right from the beginning, but I was unsure about her true identity. After a couple of weeks, she agreed to come hang out at my place, but when she arrived, several people kept calling her, and it was then that she revealed to me that she had to go to work as an escort. I can't say I was shocked because I already felt she was doing something of that nature, so why did I ignore it?

If a man's sexual desire were removed, he might ignore the manipulative tactics of a sex worker, but since that's nearly impossible, sex remains a traded commodity. For those lacking discipline in this area, loneliness and depression become common companions, and the only way to avoid these feelings is by engaging in work that truly matters to them. I once dated an adult content creator during a depressive spell, and initially, I didn't pay much attention to her profession until I started feeling better; that's when my disgust arose. I reflected on the men who watched her and what she might have done for the right price. I also thought about the types of men she allowed into her energy space and how that energy could influence me. This awareness diminished my sexual desire — she sensed the negativity, and surprisingly, she responded with increased affection as my energy pushed her away.

Her increased desire for me seemed rooted in the idea of wanting what's unobtainable. I could ignore her energy because I saw it as open-source rather than proprietary. Some people with open-source energy become popular and profit from it. Yet, when it involves sexual energy, it should only be proprietary if linked to emotional thoughts that connect to the Light Realm. Would you prefer your energy source code to be freely accessible for anyone to view, alter, and share, or to have restricted subscription access? Many men believe they would handle open-source energy well, so they suppress negative feelings until, at a restaurant, a stranger approaches her like a fan—the day before their wedding!

If you haven't realized it by now, this also applies to adult content creators working online who think that because they aren't doing stuff in person, it's an exception. Going back to the woman I mentioned, she allowed me to say sexual things I would never say to a normal girl, but the thing that struck me the most was the opinions of her from regular women I kept encountering. What I didn't mention was that even though I subconsciously knew what she did, I still wanted to engage with her as long as she took a shower beforehand. The only thing that stopped me was the random critique from a regular but good woman I spoke to on the phone at work, who randomly told me she divorced her husband after finding out he went to Mexico and slept with a sex worker; now she was happily remarried, while he's still struggling. Now that I think back on this, the Light Realm put this woman on my path.

I didn't encounter that adult content creator by chance. It was because of what I was doing during my most private moments that she appeared in my energetic path. At that time, I was struggling with loneliness, so I turned to adult content to fill that void. Although I knew deep down it was wrong, I would watch it a few times weekly without realizing it was steering me into a difficult thought pattern. I met many women, but each had a dark trait that made me reflect on my own character. It's important to understand that digest isn't just a word; it's about the feelings your subconscious actions convey, revealing what's hidden beneath the surface. When others detect this and respond negatively through non-verbal cues, it's your choices in those private moments that are to blame.

The true power of the dark energy realm lies in its ability to manipulate what appears normal, such as politics, and direct your thoughts toward negativity. Consider this: if a salesperson tries to sell you something unnecessary, you'd typically walk away. However, if they create a need and compliment something about you, they gain access to your emotions. Once you're in an emotional state, the same salesperson's attempt to upsell you on something you don't need becomes more effective because you've developed an emotional connection to their sales pitch rather than your own needs.

As stated before, your feelings and emotions are either open source or proprietary, so I review whatever is in my foyer before it comes in. I once had a friend from another country who wanted to be a singer but got heavily involved in politics. The last time I saw him, it was like talking to a different person because his subconscious actions were creating a genuinely divisive aura that I could feel. I remember we were talking, and I pronounced a word most Blacks use among each other, but his non-verbal reaction told me he was disgusted with how I used it. I used the word again later, and he corrected me. I then explained that most Black people say that word among themselves, but instead of acknowledging our cultural difference, he became even angrier. I wondered why an immigrant who speaks a different language and dialect would be so put off by a culture he knows little about. I thought to myself, if I wanted to learn about his culture, I would simply ask rather than be repulsed by it. This made me realize he was losing the battle to the dark energy force.

Disgust is one of those emotions that doesn't really need words and can cross all sorts of cultural boundaries. Even if you try to hide it, your body language will usually give you away. It's totally okay to feel disgusted by certain foods or drinks that aren't your taste, but if you're disgusted on a cultural level, it might lead to negative feelings. In Los Angeles, there's a place called Skid Row, which some see as filled with disgust—though it's not necessarily about smell or appearance. Instead, it's more about how many people there seem to have lost their sense of purpose. Everyone is born with a calling to serve others and shine their light. If you choose to ignore that calling, you might find yourself drifting on autopilot, away from your true purpose.

Envy

Wow, this might be the most exciting part so far. This word is so deeply connected to dark energy that it keeps your emotions trapped in negative thought patterns, leading nowhere. When I think of this word, feelings of depression come up, followed by anger, then back to depression. It clings to you like a tick, and before you know it, you're paralyzed. Honestly, I don't know how to fight this, but I guess you should find something you love about yourself and use growth techniques to lift yourself up instead of pulling yourself down. Growing up, my brothers and I had different skin tones — two lighter and two darker. I remember my mom pointing that out sometimes, but it wasn't just her; we also heard it at school. What's known as colorism has been and remains a major divide.

Before diving into the internal conflict of colorism within the American Black community, let's first look at North and South Korea. It would be racist to say all Koreans look alike, but generally, their facial features and skin tones seem more similar compared to two American Blacks who look completely different, like Barack Obama and Wesley Snipes. For envy to exist, one group must feel inferior to the other, and with this idea alone, we all find ourselves in this mental space. This is the thought process we all navigate on our way to understanding, wherever we are. This is the hatred that hate breeds, but I believe the next paragraphs present a solution.

Growing up in a low-income neighborhood, we also found ourselves at the bottom of the social hierarchy. My mother never needed to explain this to us directly; it was clear from how the other kids behaved. I remember a neighbor with a grandson who visited during the summer but was never allowed to play outside with us, claiming he couldn't go beyond the front steps. My brother and I thought he was cool, so whenever his grandmother told us he was visiting, we'd go to the door and hang out on the porch. One time, we tried to knock, but he didn't want to talk, and when we knocked again, his grandmother said he couldn't speak because he had chores. Months later, we saw him walking in, and when we approached, he joked, "Hey, some kids said y'all were poor." I believed him wholeheartedly, but my younger brother knew he'd made up the story to show he was better off. Why did his superior attitude toward me blind me so much?

Hate, as both a verb and a noun, signifies an intense dislike for something. Therefore, "dislike" indicates negative emotions, with envy being one of them. Examining the roots of emotions shows they are formed through experiences, and people can't genuinely say they have a choice about these experiences. As we all know, plans often don't go as expected. For example, when I enlisted in the military at nineteen, I had no idea I would want to become an officer. Still, it eventually became a goal, leading me to start attending night classes to pursue it. Because I sustained many injuries, the goal of becoming a uniformed officer never materialized; however, during my civil service career, I did become a contracting officer, which involved advising senior officers on business matters.

Anyone who has enlisted in the military knows that becoming an officer is a rare achievement for prior enlisted members. While advancing in ranks is always significant, arriving at a higher rank than your friends, especially after joining together, can trigger feelings of envy. Seeing a peer get promoted or reach a higher status can't be avoided. I remember working on my officer application with a guy I played basketball with, sharing updates along the way. We both got rejected from Navy OCS, but he decided to try the Army instead. In just three months, he was an officer, while I was still waiting to hear about new billets from my recruiter. When I saw him walk into the gym with that gold bar, envy hit me hard—I was unusually silent afterwards.

Envy might seem like a negative emotion at first, but what's truly noteworthy about it is how it shapes your character. I longed for that gold medal on my chest, just like my friend, but I let my emotions control my experiences instead of letting my experiences influence my feelings. I needed to realize that I couldn't achieve my goal exactly as I imagined; if I could, I would go back before birth and plan the best routes to a successful life. I started to think about my basketball buddy, who earned his gold medal by marketing himself as a product with multiple uses. I knew that was the key to drawing from the positive emotional pool when you feel knee-deep in negativity.

Hollywood can sometimes feel like a place where dreams fade, as many arrive hopeful but end up caught in a cycle of negativity. I don't usually see myself as an author since writing a book wasn't really part of my plan—though I do enjoy casually jotting down thoughts on my phone. Just before I started writing this, my life took a difficult turn—I lost my girlfriend, and my Hollywood connections gradually stopped reaching out, as if their subconscious somehow sensed my time in California was ending. These events pushed me to watch videos of people on Skid Row and research more affordable places in other states. Even with my recent degree in screenwriting, I felt like I was failing, and I realize now how dangerous that kind of thinking can be. In these moments, it's so important to remember that setbacks don't define us, and there's always a way forward.

I was sitting there at 2 am, observing a guy ride through Skid Row and the notorious Figueroa Street, when it hit me to turn off my phone and concentrate on meaningful, productive ideas. Let me clarify that: I turned off my phone and sat in the dark, pondering the best ideas I could generate, which led to the thought of writing this book. I suspect that if I asked people in Skid Row, most would say they lost everything, but few would mention how their attitude fostered a hostile work environment—ultimately causing them to get fired or quit. My mother never attended college, only earning a GED, yet she held desk jobs and even thrived in the high-tech industry because of her attitude. She never complained about her coworkers or criticized their character; she was simply a joy to be around and remains so. As for me, I never lost or quit a job due to my performance; it was always my attitude that resulted in living out of my car.

I never imagined I'd become homeless, but when it happened, I found myself in a situation you might understand. Gyms became my showers, the car served as my living space, and my sanity was fragile. Interestingly, even in such circumstances, a small spark of hope—like a white energy ball—continues to grow; it seems as if people feel more connected. It's a feeling reminiscent of childhood, when emotions are pure and simple. Kids do experience envy and other negative feelings, but their thoughts aren't as complex as during adolescence and beyond. I recall the first time I felt envy: when my best friend got the girl I liked, and I thought he only did because his parents bought him new clothes each year. Despite him getting her, I don't remember envy turning into hate. It wasn't until high school that I realized envy and hate are often close companions.

High school is a place full of different experiences, and you'll either love it or hate it. My first two years in high school were spent hanging out with troublemakers because I saw myself that way. The so-called bad kids didn't have nice clothes and weren't in extracurricular activities because of financial struggles, so I fit right in. It would be foolish to tell you I committed crimes just to pay for haircuts, so I'll just say I never did anything I felt was wrong, but I knew where to draw the line. I can say I never sold drugs because I understood how drugs can affect a household, but everything else was possible. During that time, I had many run-ins with law enforcement. It was like they knew I was up to no good but couldn't prove it.

I remember coming up with a plan to get some money from people on their payday. But on the day, I was planning to go through with it, I was unexpectedly pulled over because of something hanging from my rearview mirror that blocked my view. To make things even more surprising, I found out that a relative of mine had been jailed for the same thing I was thinking about doing. And to top it off, I saw my friend from the Projects heading to court for the same crime. This just shows how the Thought Lanes I talk about aren't just about us; they involve others, too. Some, like the Police, are there to remind us, give us a ticket, or even take us to jail.

It became clear that the Universe was guiding me away from this crime, showing me a real-time view of the beginning, middle, and end of my plan. Because I saw these events unfold, I decided not to go through with it. It made me wonder, though: if these things happened to me and I chose to give up, why are so many people in jail or prison? Is the Universe only helping certain individuals it considers worthy of the Light Realm?

When you think of someone who is envied, who comes to mind? I used to think of professional basketball players because I knew they often dated the most attractive girls in school. If the universe gives you a 6-foot-6 height with above-average athletic skills, why wouldn't you choose basketball? Even without basketball, a 6-foot-6 man is usually envied because women tend to prefer taller men. Now, you have a situation where the shorter man feels negatively about his height, while the taller man walks confidently, yet neither wants to settle for less than the best. Envy comes from feeling entitled to what you lack, so counter that by reminding yourself that you are just renting who you are. I know this sounds strange, but if you imagine a version of yourself that's exactly how you want to be, you'll begin to see the benefits of drawing from the positive pool that leads to the Light Realm.

As this book approaches the end, I find myself envying authors more for their dedication in turning an idea from a concept into a tangible product that people can purchase. Many would say that this kind of envy is harmless, since the underlying feeling is more about motivational jealousy. If you haven't noticed, we haven't talked about jealousy until now.

At the dawn of humanity, Homo sapiens needed something to keep them warm, so at some point, fire was invented. Somewhere along the way, another person discovered that animal fur could provide warmth, leading to the development of a process for making a coat. I'm sure others observed this and wanted to learn how it was done, and I believe that information was shared, but it wasn't until the scarcity of animals arose that feelings of jealousy started to surface. Fast forward to modern times—someone created digital currencies as a way to exchange goods and services, so now everyone wants a piece of the action. Yet, nothing has changed when it comes to someone recognizing a need in the world, developing a concept, and evaluating whether others want it; this is the science of business. So, if people understand the science of business, what's with all the jealousy?

Unfortunately, the business science I discussed is much more challenging because of the competition, which is deeply rooted in jealousy. I once wrote a TV pilot about an unmarried man who created a billion-dollar product and decided to start his own town. The first 100 people in his town received an acre of land, livestock, a home, and $100,000. To grow the town, anyone wanting to become a citizen needed a unanimous vote. Once accepted, they were required to contribute $1000 to any new resident so they could receive land, livestock, a home, and $100,000. After a few years, the town, now the size of a state, was thriving, and millions of applications poured in. At one point, the town stopped accepting applications because it couldn't keep up with demand, which made many nearby cities furious. They decided to take action against this so-called utopian society, so instead of trying to create a similar town, other towns declared war, with thousands dying because of envy.

The story you just read highlights a reality many face today: it's often easier to be drawn toward dark thoughts than toward light ones. Why is this? When viewed through a powerful telescope, the universe appears mostly dark, hinting that we may already be living in a Dark Realm. Scientists have discovered that the universe is expanding at an accelerated rate due to a mysterious cosmic force. While this expansion might seem like progress, it actually indicates the presence of a vacuum connected to dark energy. This energy seems to aim to drain all light, gradually cooling and isolating the universe.

Some might ask, "Well, if it's a vacuum, why aren't planets being sucked away?" I'm just a simple man who doesn't have nearly the intelligence needed to be an astrophysicist, but why can't they explain to me why dreams can sometimes seem and feel real? It seems as though something inside us remains active while our bodies rest, but we'll explore that a little later. What's important to understand is that the feeling of jealousy works on behalf of the dark energy source, and recognizing that you are actively being recruited is the best way to start shifting your thoughts toward the positive pool of the Light Realm.

Fear

The word that connects us all, and probably the root of our inevitable downfall. We understand this well, and most of us can't recall the first time we felt it, but everyone has a story behind it. When I was in second grade, I struggled with reading, so the school placed me in a slow learner class down the hall. This class had many troubled kids, and mostly, a fight happened every week, but ironically, I never felt fear around them. A few months later, my mother got me glasses, and, to the teacher's surprise, I could read, so they moved me back to regular classes. I remember my mom coming to school, feeling so proud that I wasn't a challenge youth; the only thing is, I started to feel what we know as fear.

Most of the fear came from being one of the poorer kids in the class. I remember Tommy Hilfiger was a popular brand, so if you had that, you were pretty popular. My clothes were dingy, but I told myself that if I didn't say much and looked mean, no one would mess with me, and it worked. I spent all of middle school, up to the 7th grade, not saying much. In fact, in the 7th grade, I went to a school with uniforms, and my grades were so good that I made the high honor roll, but that's beside the point since I never said much.

Fear kept me silent, and by high school, I essentially became a mute—no smiles or games. I was working through a fear of humiliation over my lack of money, so silence became my strongest defense. Most popular kids chatted as they walked the hallways to each class, but my goal was to walk with my head held high without speaking. Because of this, I really disliked high school, but who could I blame? My mom was handicapped, and my dad was trying to handle his own struggles. Hope arrived when we moved from a low-income, gang-affected area to a suburban neighborhood, thanks to my Aunt and Uncle, who helped us through their connections in the electrical business.

I began connecting with some of the white guys in the neighborhood who seemed quite grounded. Many of them grew up with two parents at home and mentioned plans to go to college. Coming from a different part of town where college wasn't really on people's minds, I started to see that there was a bigger picture here.

Empathetic Pain

Have you ever seen a commercial showing a hungry child in a developing country or a young child fighting cancer and felt moved to donate? You might feel good if your money helps them, but you may wonder if the charity is being fully transparent. Feeling joy from helping others is rewarding, but why do we need to see people suffering to be motivated to help? And why do we feel threatened when the situation is reversed? Many of the modern emotions we experience are influenced by social media and politics.

As I mentioned earlier, I tend to stay neutral when it comes to politics. But it's a reality that when one side wins, the other has to lose. Republicans and Democrats both understand this all too well, and it means that this cycle continues for the next four years, leaving the losing side to feel the sting of defeat. The pain of losing can ignite some of the strongest competitive drives among people, but unfortunately, it can also contribute to increased homelessness and drug use, which are serious concerns we need to address.

In an ideal world, you'd grow up in a two-parent household where there's no arguing, bills are paid, and a nutritious, wholesome meal is served on the table every night so the family can sit, talk, and enjoy each other. This would eventually lead you to attend a great university, where you would discover both your passion and the love of your life. From there, you would repeat the same wonderful cycle for your children, creating a chain of joy through generations.

All of this is fine and dandy, except I forgot to mention the bullying you went through in high school, the STD you got from that guy you love, and the fact that you hate the career choice you made. The first story was straight out of the 1950s lifestyle program they used to promote, as it lacked emotion, while the second one is full of feelings. I've tried to avoid my emotions since the pain I felt from being rejected by my first high school crush, but to navigate through life, you have to develop these emotions or end up homeless, dead, or in prison, which, by the way, are all hubs for the dark energy force.

I want you to go out and ask a few homeless folks how they ended up in that situation. Then, tell me what emotional downfall they couldn't recover from. I once dated a girl who was absolutely beautiful, but she did drugs, and I knew from growing up that a person addicted to substances is controlled by something so strong that it takes the strongest emotions to defeat it. You see, my mother hated drugs, but her husband, my stepfather, was an addict. He was actually a hardworking guy who kept to himself, but when that drug called him, he became a totally different person, and he had a look in his eyes when he was on it that I will never forget. His drug use brought instability into our house, but on the other hand, my brothers and I knew what unconditional love truly was. I remember him putting my mother in the hospital for a few days, only for her to return a couple of months later, and nobody said a word; he was just back in our lives.

I didn't start reflecting on my feelings toward my stepfather until after I left the military, which was around the age of 24. His actions from years ago hit me hard because I was now growing into a man who wanted a relationship with a woman, causing my mind to recall scenes from my childhood. Have you ever watched those reality TV shows where they hold interventions, only to find out that the events affecting the people happened many years earlier? The question is, why are they dealing with it now? The pain can bury itself deep inside you, allowing you to feel fine for years, only to be triggered by a dream or flashback that causes the pain to erupt like a volcano! It's like something on your life timeline has to set it off, and since you can't control time, it's bound to happen whether you're ready or not.

I try to prevent painful events from flooding my thoughts by identifying what triggers them. Even though my stepfather did some crazy things while I was growing up, nothing he did compared to the trauma experienced by a kid who was molested or beaten. Most of my triggers come from comments kids made about me at school, especially regarding my clothes or lack thereof. Outside of that, my childhood was fairly normal compared to the average kid in America.

When I mention being 'normal,' I mean we've faced financial struggles—and honestly, who hasn't? For someone who has experienced hardship like being beaten or molested, maintaining the ability to steer their thoughts is so important for personal growth. One great example is music. Music has the power to evoke deep emotions and can quickly shift you from feeling on top of the world to feeling down—without you even realizing you're changing lanes.

Next time you check your playlist, take a moment to see which thought lane it's most often putting you in.

Positive	**Negative**
Admiration	Anger
Adoration	Anxiety
Aesthetic Appreciation	Awkwardness
Amusement	Boredom
Awe	Confusion
Calmness	Craving
Empathic Pain	Disgust
Entrancement	Entrancement
Excitement	Fear
Interest	Horror
Joy	Sadness
Nostalgia	Sexual Desire
Relief	
Romance	
Satisfaction	

Surprise

Notably, entrancement exists on both sides, as it can shift in either direction, which we'll explore later. It might be mostly positive or mainly negative; only you can determine the answer. My intention is to stay optimistic because I want to achieve my fullest growth potential. A few months prior to writing this book, I looked through my music playlists and found them to be quite discouraging.

Most of the lyrics conveyed feelings of desperation, loneliness, and survival, which were reflected in my daily actions and interactions. Surprisingly, I thought this was good music because I believed I was okay as long as it wasn't hardcore rap like Drill music. At that time, I heard a televangelist mention that what you put into your inner self influences what you reveal outwardly. I reasoned that allowing these feelings in would attract similar feelings back to me, like a magnet.

It's that old saying that what you put into the Universe is what you'll get out of it, but the thing is, when you listen to music or browse social media content, you're not actually putting anything into the Universe; you're following an algorithm (Thought Lane). So, the real question is, who's creating these algorithms?

The simple definition of an 'algorithm' is a finite sequence of steps that can solve a problem or complete a task. However, in everyday language, we often see it trending on social media. But what exactly is social media, especially regarding our 27 sets of emotions? This is highly subjective, so interpret it as you will, but I see it as a platform that makes communication easier. In the Middle Ages, or even as recently as the 90s, we had no way to see or hear each other without meeting face-to-face; now, a single click suffices.

Technology has made this possible, enabling marketing firms, celebrities, and the entertainment industry, among others, to exploit our need to connect. I use the word 'need' because communication is essential for our mental well-being; without it, concepts like imprisonment would be ineffective. Shakespeare's phrase "To be or not to be" reflects the choice between life and death, with death often seen as the ultimate escape from mental strain. You might not realize it, but algorithms tend to isolate us as group thinkers. We will explore this idea further in another section.

If you haven't noticed yet, empathic pain is a positive aspect, since even though pain is difficult, it's one of those rare emotions that, when experienced mutually, can motivate two or more people to seek positive feelings. I once heard a story about a teenager who murdered another teenager and was incarcerated for a long time. During his sentence, the victim's mother reached out to the killer, and when they met, they both wept. After he was released, he started a non-profit to encourage youths against gun violence. These two individuals shared the same pain but on opposite ends of the spectrum, and because they chose to empathize, their message to both young and old people carries a more meaningful impact. Because our need for community exists, pain will happen. However, choosing to empathize and sympathize with feelings outside our own, while deciding to focus on positive thoughts, will guide us toward the Light Realm.

Horror

Are you thinking of the same movie I am right now? Luckily, this may be the only feeling that belongs on television, but for those who have experienced horror stories, I'd suggest writing a book and making a movie to cope with it.

I have several organic movies playing at once, and I experience them as dreams. In one of my dreams, I never left my home state and never became a Contracting Officer. Instead, I stayed as an Enlisted person, struggling to get my degree while working for several Officers, one of whom makes me salute him indoors just because he knows he can.

This version of me gives me nightmares, and although I know it's just a dream, I still feel the horror during it and for several minutes after I wake up. Do you dream at all? Can you relate to me about these kinds of dreams?

Although the last sentence of the final paragraph might seem rhetorical, if we meet in person, I'd like to hear your answer, as it could be the key to whether you're living the best version of yourself within your subconscious experiences.

<u>Sadness</u>

You may or may not realize this, but sadness is not the same as depression; if it were, one of these words wouldn't exist. It's important to understand that sadness is a fleeting emotion, while depression is more persistent. For example, if you don't get a good score on your SAT or ACT, you'll feel sad but have the option to retake the test or work at a warehouse stacking boxes on the back of a truck. Eventually, stacking those boxes will take a toll on your back, and you'll find a way to get into college unless you meet the love of your life at the warehouse—which is a different story.

Anyway, sadness is a temporary feeling that doesn't cause a chemical imbalance, but it can if you let it. I have a friend whose dog died a few years ago, and I can tell it affects her, especially when we're out and she sees other people with their dogs. The same thing happens when we lose loved ones; you think about not being able to call, text, or see them. Sadness visits you, but the great moments you all shared make the sadness even deeper.

Sometimes, it's necessary to let tears flow at night to help make the days better. A close friend of mine recently lost her father, who was everything to her and her children. It's important to find gratitude for the time spent together. I never had the chance to know my grandparents, so I didn't have a strong emotional attachment, but I do remember the few good moments we shared, and I think about those to feel better.

Walking around feeling sad all the time can create a negative vibe, and naturally, people might want to stay away. Remember, having low energy, self-esteem, and confidence issues are often choices we make in our minds. So, why not embrace the chance to change today, moment by moment? Just imagine how much love and positivity the Light Realm could shower you with if you shift your energy with your thoughts!

Entrancement

The fascination with politics has led society in a negative direction. I recall walking into a room full of young white American adults when I overheard one of them say they were more progressive. As they noticed me, everyone fell silent, waiting for my non-verbal response. I didn't do anything but keep walking because, in my view, politics has somehow become a covert way of judging who is racist and who isn't, and that was his way of signaling that he was okay with Blacks.

Today, conservatives argue that progressives only show warmth to Black voters during elections, then revert to distancing themselves once the votes are counted. It might seem absurd if I said I was going to adopt a white person's perspective, but if I walk into a room of a hundred white people wearing this permanent black makeup, all of them would surely be curious about which thought lane I belong to—especially if confidential information is being exchanged.

I've lived in California for several years, but before I moved here, I thought this place would be highly advanced with super-smart and tech-savvy people. Don't get me wrong, California definitely fits that description, but as a Black American observing other Black Americans, I would say that the dominant culture hinders intellectual growth. What I mean by this is that there's more focus on gang culture than on intellectual pursuits. We often hear about a superiority complex, but what about an inferiority complex?

As an educated and articulate Black man living in this state, I often face cryptic comments and non-verbal cues from non-Blacks, which leave me frustrated. Why should I bear the negative cultural stereotypes when I haven't exhibited those traits? Also, please clarify the box you just placed me in because I wasn't aware I was supposed to be in one. I can only assume that the demand-driven algorithm has significantly influenced all of our subconscious thoughts.

There are many intelligent Black people, but I wonder when society will consider it normal to distinguish the entertaining characters they see online from the reliable expertise of a local doctor they might meet.

I'm not saying they don't, but if you walk into your doctor's appointment and see a black person with an accent you dislike, you'd probably find a way to leave and never come back, and that applies to any race.

Society's judgment based on appearance will continue because the standard look has already been set. I believe this unfairly disadvantages talented individuals. I do appreciate that some social media algorithms highlight content, like videos of doctors who don't look like the typical medical professional but are just as skilled. They seem to accept this diversity, but we need to start seeing it as normal in everyday life. For example, if someone aspires to be a doctor and excels academically but looks like a rapper, will society accept that when they visit a clinic? Or will they unconsciously expect to see someone who fits the ingrained mental image?

In modern business, leading marketing firms utilize psychographics to target potential customers based on their attitudes, lifestyles, values, and interests rather than just race and gender. This strategy centers on understanding how people feel. For instance, I challenge you to ask a young person why they chose their outfit. They might not care until you suggest it's typical for Generation Z, which often triggers defensiveness. This inner conflict reflects an evolutionary trait that examines categorical feelings, often pigeonholing us as a society. I want to highlight that early on, thought paths were limited, but as countless experiences accumulated, new thought lanes emerged. To optimize human resources, we must leverage psychographics; otherwise, people risk following thought pathways that lead nowhere.

As I write this, I am in my mid-30s, having experienced life before the advent of social media and now living in a world where it is everywhere. If I imagine myself in the thought pattern of a black male Millennial based on internet search results, I appear to be highly educated, well-dressed, and articulate. Comparing these results to those of an average white male Millennial in society, would I find myself in the same thought lane, or would realistic distractions steer me elsewhere? These results don't seem to match perfectly; otherwise, prison yards and subsidized housing wouldn't be so populated with Blacks. While I hope most of my peers are highly educated, well-dressed, and articulate, the algorithm's competitive tactics and our subconscious biases often lead to a different outcome.

I once signed up for a 5:30 cycling class in Redlands, CA, wanting to try something new outside basketball and running. However, I encountered a collective subconscious mindset. Trying something new is driven by interest, but there are gateway energy holders that allow or deny entry based on collective energy, not physical presence. In the class, most participants were my age, yet I felt held back by the music choice. As a Black male, the group defaulted to thinking I only liked rap, even though my favorite genre is electro dance music. The instructor mentioned feeling pressured choosing music, and a guy behind me laughed, suggesting a shared subconscious assumption that I was only into rap. Was this subconscious bias racially driven against my music preferences?

While I appreciate rap music's significant influence on the economic and social empowerment of the black community, it comes with a tradeoff—the presence of a default subconscious Unimind. As I mentioned earlier, I observed this phenomenon in Redlands, CA. Despite Redlands being a charming middle-to-upper-class area, it borders San Bernardino, a city that has long fallen behind in reputation due to ongoing gang violence, low-income housing, and a homeless population, especially as of 2025. Although the city is predominantly Hispanic, many black residents live there, a fact I only discovered after my cycling class. I was trying to understand the root cause of this default collective subconscious Unimind, rather than assuming that Redlands is filled with subtle racists who judge me because I like rap music. After that class, I wondered: if I grew up in San Bernardino and took that cycling class out of interest, would I have even done it?

I wouldn't have taken that class because it made me think about my hometown of Joliet, IL, and a nearby town called Plainfield, IL, where I knew the same gateway energy holders were present as in Redlands. Despite my military service and education, I believed these gateway energy holders might have judged me based on where I grew up, and I realize that my thoughts on this need to change. I hope you don't interpret this as me claiming my thought patterns are perfect or as an attempt to tell you how to think—this isn't my intention. My goal is to raise awareness of the entrancements our collective subconscious can fall into so we can better understand and navigate our interactions with others.

Unfortunately, I cannot effectively change others' subconscious perceptions of my music preferences or make the girl with the attractive organic peach become more aware of me because I'm black. I can only focus on maintaining the most positive thoughts at that moment to keep moving toward the Light Realm. Suppose you want something so badly and know it puts you in a positive emotional pool. In that case, conflict might initially persist with the energy gateholders, but once they sense your desire to become whatever it is, don't be surprised by what happens next.

Sexual Desire

When you hear the words "sexual" or "sex," what image appears in your mind? It might be a specific person or a particular moment, but whatever you're thinking of that distracts you from these words provides insight into your subatomic self within the parent sexual desire thought lane. Sex itself isn't negative; in fact, without it, humanity wouldn't exist.

When I think about sex, I immediately associate it with how women communicate with me through eye contact and how powerful that look feels. However, I once made eye contact with a guy who gave me a similar look, but internally I rejected it. For him — whom I assume is gay — showing non-verbal, in-person interest seems to be the first step toward any sexual interaction. So, why did the Universe make him gay while giving me heterosexual instincts? The Universe's methods of balancing its systems for sensual ecological capacity remain a mystery, but if I had to guess, it tries to matchmake within certain subconscious groups. But is it actually working?

How often do we see two people who seem like a perfect match turn out to be a nightmare? More often than expected, right? My mother and stepfather are an example, but I always knew they shared strong sexual chemistry. When I was younger, I struggled to distinguish between infatuation and genuine interest in a girl, and I can tell you that this remains difficult today. It's hard to separate her physical appeal from her inner qualities, like values, beliefs, and interests. How can I focus on truly understanding her if her physical attributes are exaggerated or if her assets don't match her liabilities? Even better, what if she lacks the qualities needed for a genuine connection, so we can both have a memorable night? Let me share a story from my very first experience.

I want to clarify that my first sexual experience was with protection, so it doesn't count; I didn't know her name and barely remember what she looked like, and no feelings were involved. We'll move on. I first met my "first time" at her office during a medical visit. When she entered, I felt attracted to her, but there was no strong sexual chemistry. Since I was somewhat attracted, we stayed connected initially, and everything remained friendly. Then she made a sexual overture by asking if my package was average or above average. This was notable because I wasn't thinking of her sexually until she asked—otherwise, I would have kept the interaction purely platonic. After learning her name, we started dating and meeting up, and eventually she invited me to her home. Being invited to a woman's home usually means I've passed the high-stakes round, but for me, it felt like I was just visiting a friend—and that's where I went wrong.

Our first sexual experience was disappointing for me but satisfying for her. Right afterward, she told me she didn't think my "ego" was big enough because I was so nice, and I believed being a nice guy was what got me that far. You see, the Universe was working in her favor because I knew deep down, I wasn't sexually attracted to her, so this was being revealed to her by my subconscious "ego" thought process. I only performed well because I would think about another girl I was attracted to to boost my performance, but I was never able to finish. My inability to finish didn't concern her, since a lot of pre-ejaculate was present, but she kept asking if I had finished after each encounter, so now the Universe was coming for me. The truth was, I was a fraud, but because she was a decent person and someone I thought would be a great mom, I kept up the act, but boy, I didn't know what was coming.

Because I couldn't release with her, I still felt the urge to do so afterward, so I would usually wait until she was either asleep or when I was distant from her to release. There was a specific type of girl I thought of during sex with her and also during my release. This type of girl started physically appearing everywhere I went: grocery stores, car washes, retail shops, and many other places, to name a few. Since I was a respectful boyfriend, I never approached or made eye contact with any of them, as I felt I was already with the girl I was meant to be with.

After a couple of months, I got used to my before-and-after routine with her, and she even said she was okay with me doing it because she was getting her release, so that's all that mattered. One day, I came home from work and she was reading a book. When I asked her where she got it from, she said it just appeared on her desk with a note from one of her customers. I had no idea this book would be the start of the end of my fraudulent ways.

I haven't provided a description of the person I was dating because I wanted you to understand the backstory, not my intentions. Remember when I mentioned she invited me to her house and I felt like I was visiting a friend? That was the moment when the Universe began ensuring that a particular book reached her—possibly to protect her from me. Our relationship ended because that book explicitly states that if a man isn't releasing, he's faking it with you. After that, our relationship started to fall apart; she even dreamt about the specific girl I was thinking of. I didn't realize it then, but the book that found me was working in her favor, in mine, and most importantly, in yours.

Insecurity is the most powerful feeling linked to sexual desire. What can someone do about being too short, too tall, hair loss, poor eyesight, missing parts, short or long "parts," their voice, eye color, skin tone, hair texture, and weight, to name a few? Religious groups say we were made in His image. Even though I think this refers to other beings that don't look like humans out in the Universe, why do people get plastic surgery? Most men who feel they lack height and good looks try to find comfort in their income, hoping to attract the same number of women. But what I'm about to share will end all of that because good women are the true driving force in life, and their nature will determine how much power we, as a collective, give to the mysterious yet dark energy force.

My mother is one of the most joyful-spirited people I've ever known. I've never seen her depressed, angered without reason, self-critical, or bitter about life's challenges; it's just not in her nature. My father, meanwhile, is quite a character. I've seen him unleash his anger, especially while driving. As a kid, I found his habit of telling other drivers how they should drive hilarious. When he saw someone doing something wrong, he would curse at them and then pull up to the light for a stare-down, but for some reason, the other driver never wanted, in the vernacular, "that smoke." As I grew older and faced adult issues, I began doing the same, but I was more angry and willing to risk everything. I remember driving one day, listening to hardcore rap, when a pedestrian illegally crossed the street. I stopped, rolled down my window, and cursed at him. To my surprise, he didn't turn around; he just kept walking, which made me even angrier. Even though I knew I was tapping into a dark energy, I wondered why I couldn't control it like my father did in the car.

I want to share that my father spent several years in prison, which completely changed our family's life path. Before his incarceration, he was a military veteran with a steady job, but his inability to control his anger led him to be imprisoned at different times. He often told me that because he had gone to prison for my sake, I should focus on becoming a man and starting a family so they wouldn't have to know about any of that. You might ask, "What does this have to do with sexual desire?" What you need to understand is that my mother's nature reflects the typical attitude of women, seeing their role as nurturing. When my mother allowed my dad to express his sexual desires with her, his role was to protect and provide for her and the children she might have. To his credit, he fulfilled that for several years, but eventually, he fell into negative thought patterns. She, as a good woman, stepped back and pulled us away from him to protect us. My father still had sexual desires, so he found another woman, and her, sadly, was the reason he ended up in prison for five years, which drastically changed our family's course. Do you now see the importance of having a good woman versus a bad one?

Regardless of your sexual orientation, if your sexual desire for your person of interest doesn't lead to mutual feelings of love, you're on a thought lane drawn from dark energy. I'll say this once more: if your desire isn't reciprocated with love, you're on a thought lane pulling from dark energy. The Universe, as an entity, has created countless thought lanes with trillions of routes for human experiences, but it has inherently given every conscious being two main feelings: love and hate. Just look at the animal kingdom—while a key predator like a wolf or lion can kill whenever they want, it's usually to satisfy hunger, not ambition. If they started killing for thrill, more powerful animals like elephants would step in and eliminate them to maintain ecological balance. Applying this to humans, the *Star Wars* character Darth Vader became too ambitious, and the people he loved most became the force to stop him. The question is, what makes him, my dad, and others who enter opposing thought lanes dismiss their feelings as if they are amoral?

Characters like Darth Vader and Marvel's Thanos thought they were bringing balance to the universe by arbitrarily controlling people's behavior. They overlooked the key factor that governs behavior: the inability to control how people feel. Without this, we wouldn't understand what true freedom is. But what is sexual freedom? Perhaps it's the ability to have a one-night stand every weekend until you find the right partner, or to visit places where prostitution is legal and try something new each night. Sexual freedom is available to everyone, but it comes with a significant cost linked to dark energy. I avoid mentioning celebrity names, but there's a well-known, influential woman who rose to fame because of a sex tape. She didn't expect it to be widely circulated, yet it greatly boosted her income, now exceeding a billion dollars. Even today, if she stands beside a man, most assume she's sleeping with him. Because of her wealth, fame, and perceived promiscuity, she can't do normal or even public dating without facing judgment. Additionally, the man she believes to be her true love and the father of her children continues to challenge her understanding of family—something she grew up believing. Therefore, the cost of giving in to sexual desires exceeds the perceived benefits. Despite her sharp business acumen and kind, affectionate nature, she still has to deal with what I call symptoms of the dark energy force.

Even though we don't know the origin or nature of dark energy, we can assume it behaves like water, seeking its own level to keep the universe free of Light Energy. Since it can't consume everything in the universe on its own, it uses symptoms to produce more dark energy to pursue its goal. For example, the Influential TV personality I mentioned before has the same sexual needs as anyone else, but the dark energy force recognized that it could use her as a vessel to further its cause by promoting the idea that being sexually desired is acceptable, even if she herself does not believe it. Demand for plastic surgery has increased because more people want to be more sexually desirable. As a man, I can tell you these surgeries are working because when I first started seeing these enhanced women online, several of my zippers broke. It was hard to tell if I was falling in love or just infatuated. Even though my eyes saw that glory, the cost was paid with the person I was dating.

At the start of one of my relationships, I was off social media, but then dark energy particles began to influence me through my wandering eye. Our sex life was good, but after I downloaded a popular social media app, she started noticing the change. I should mention that the girl I was dating was beautiful, and I genuinely thought she would make a perfect mom. However, because the symptoms of the dark energy aimed to direct my actions toward its own goal, it did whatever it needed to keep me in a negative thought pattern.

This energy force knew that secretly gazing at certain women when I was away from her would impair my performance in bed. It also fed on this by guiding us to places where I would encounter women like that and desire them more than the woman beside me. Furthermore, it made me more aggressive and angry because I couldn't have what my subconscious was feeding into, which eventually led to our breakup. We can all assume that a person who fully succumbs to their sexual desires—sleeping with anyone for any reason—has given in to this dark energy. However, the symptoms I described are typical for the average person, so it's essential to pay close attention to what triggers these conflicting thoughts.

What's a natural way to fulfill our desires while avoiding dark energy? I suggest removing the word "sexual" and focusing on what truly gives your life meaning. It could be anything that helps you draw on positive energy and support others. For example, if you explore natural resources and find ways to teach or learn how to build, use, or maintain them, you're on the right track. Another example is an exotic dancer who studies mathematics or reviews IRS publications at IRS.gov to help others — that embodies moving toward the Light Realm.

Everything depends on intent because that's how both the Light and Dark Realms evaluate your energy. If I analyze the two scenarios—one where the Exotic Dancer is a credit card scammer and another where someone develops technology to extract Earth's natural resources for personal greed—wouldn't you agree that the symptoms of dark energy are winning in their cases? The same applies to an artist who creates a popular song with millions of views but promotes sexual desire. Do you think that an artist's music encourages people to pursue thoughts that foster healthy relationships or destructive ones? Remember, conscious thoughts are like the train we see and are in, while subconscious thoughts are the railway we're traveling—so the question is, where is your energy flowing?

Getting To The Light Realm

Good news: You're nearly finished with this book! Congratulations on reaching this point. I understand that reading can be challenging with personal time constraints, and since you're doing this outside of class, it means a lot. I want to finish by encouraging you to reflect on positive experiences from your better emotional side, leading to a satisfying conclusion. Even though these are my examples, I encourage you to think of your own thoughts to evoke positive feelings anytime. As I mentioned earlier, I designed this to help you engage with your thoughts to support such feelings, so keep that in mind now and in the future.

Admiration

Who is the first person you remember making you laugh uncontrollably? Was it a parent, sibling, close friend, or someone you're dating? For me, it was my dad. A natural comedian, he mastered punchlines, mimicked mannerisms, and used voice inflections every time. His humor created many shared moments that helped fill the void when he was sent away. I grew up with three brothers, two with different fathers. My younger brother and I mostly had our dad present from early years until around age twelve or thirteen.

During those years, he taught us to cook, stay cool, and keep things fun, which is probably why my mom loved him so much. A situation eventually forced him to leave the house, but he continued to visit and talk to us, something my mother permitted. These conversations played a role in shaping who I am today. This is why I believe that admiration begins with anyone who brings positive feelings into your life, regardless of the shared moments. I can recall many mistakes he made while growing up, but dwelling on them only brings back old feelings. People grow and often know more than we do. That's why I believe it's important to evaluate others based on their personal growth to find reasons to admire them. But how can you do this if you don't know what they have going on?

Start by complimenting them and then asking a general question; this naturally creates a positive vibe. I've realized everyone has a story if you just ask. Once, I met a Jewish man in a retail store who shared how he was treated not only as a Jew but also as a northerner living in the South during his military service, and I could empathize with him. During our conversation, others joined us, and instead of feeling annoyed, we both felt proud to sit there and talk openly in public as a perceived Black man and a White man. That was one of my best encounters, but I can't count how many times attempts to connect with strangers from different backgrounds failed. Most people are friendly and will smile, but many quickly find a way to walk away from me, which is cool because I know they'll remember me for the effort at least. I will say that trying to make friends across cultural boundaries comes at a greater cost than expected.

As someone who respects other cultures, I see crossing cultural boundaries like a driver sees yellow broken lines on the road—meaning to proceed with caution, but I still cross. As a kid, we moved several times, so I would arrive at a new school and automatically be the quiet kid to avoid teasing. However, after a while, being silent became boring, so I started initiating conversations to seem cool. To my surprise, this approach worked, but at the same time, I received more criticism and, consequently, rejection from my own perceived culture. For example, I was very interested in learning more about Islam, so I visited a nearby mosque and was intrigued by the fact that they didn't eat pork and how modestly their women dressed. They also told me that the word Muslim means "One who believes in God," so I shared this with some family members, and of course, they linked my interest to their own perceptions. Because in their eyes, I wasn't just a guy showing interests in Islam; I was a Black Muslim from a radical sect.

Even now, some members of my family still think I'm a pro-black militant because of my appreciation for certain aspects of Islamic culture. Naturally, none of them have asked me directly; they just assume that's my mindset, which seems to subtly think white people are evil. However, as I've gone to university and worked on multimillion-dollar contracts alongside some of the top engineers in the country during my time with the United States Space Force, I can confirm that my admiration for innovative thinkers goes beyond anything else. The entire system of Science and Mathematics is about solving problems of the world we live in. Consider all the creative minds that developed the technology allowing you to hear and see these words without me speaking them to you in person - isn't that incredible?

Have you ever driven through a town and started seeing huge homes, wondering what those people do for a living? Whatever they did, it involved either creating or maintaining a product or service that generated high market demand. It takes years for a family to become enriched with degree'd cousins, uncles, and relatives alike. Still, the admiration usually starts with one individual in the family who not only believed in their idea but also made the sacrifice to bring it to life. So, where does one start with the idea? For me, I reviewed the North American Industry Classification System (NAICS) and scrolled through all the sectors to determine which one interested me the most. I delved further into Sector 71, "Arts, Entertainment, Recreation." I developed a plan to become a Writer, seeing that I knew the Small Business Administration recognizes NAICS codes for individuals wanting to start a business. Many people perceive business as daunting, but it's essentially just providing a product or service to others, like any other salesman you encounter. If your product or service is good, people will come back to you regardless of what you look like.

I grew up in American Black culture, which is deeply connected to Hip Hop and Rap music. Black Americans may not speak our own language like many foreigners who migrate to the United States for better opportunities, but we have our own unique dialect. This dialect has given us an economic edge, especially in the music industry.

Many Black Americans recognize that our unique subcultural English serves as a covert way to express our identity. However, in corporate settings, this kind of dialect is often deemed unacceptable. I don't view this rejection as ethnocentrism; rather, I see it as a standard for corporate communication. Essentially, if my lawyer spoke like my favorite rapper, I might not trust them with my legal documents unless their background proved otherwise. Conversely, if my favorite rapper sounded like my lawyer, I'm uncertain I'd buy their record. Our voices' tone and dialect connect us on conscious and subconscious levels. Even if someone speaks another language, I can often detect their emotion through tone. Despite different backgrounds, we speak a common language — and a word can subtly and subconsciously express admiration for my culture, creating a quiet yet meaningful link between us.

Imagine growing up as a child, eating your grandmother's favorite dish. This dish was once known only within your family and a few locals, but then someone decided to share it beyond your community. Soon, it became a worldwide phenomenon, appreciated culturally across the globe. I remember seeing a middle-aged white man in a luxury sedan pull up beside me at a traffic light, with one hand on the wheel, seat reclined, playing rap music. He nodded at me, and I nodded back — a gesture of cultural appreciation. Another time, I explained an acquisition plan to top engineers and acquisition specialists for an upcoming space launch in a confident manner, which earned their applause — another form of cultural admiration. I believe our brain, with about 86 billion neurons, allows us to learn various languages, dialects, and tones. So, why not use a small part of that capacity to better adapt to our environment? To me, this is reading the room and being genuine in real-time and in a real way.

Adoration

When was the last time you entered a room and felt genuinely loved by everyone there, without it being your birthday or a special occasion? Usually, people only get noticed when they do something to stand out, except for celebrities and attractive women. Now, imagine entering that same room with an invisible shield around you that can block or receive non-verbal signals. Would you turn it off to see what others are sending, or keep it on, ending up sitting at the bar either way? I usually keep my shield down to lessen the emotional energy directed at me. For instance, once I entered a bar, only an older man noticed me initially. I naturally approached him, but he clearly didn't want to talk. A few minutes later, a beautiful bartender came out, smiled, and asked what I wanted to drink. Through peripheral vision, I saw that this was the real reason he didn't want me to sit at the bar.

I respected the fact that he probably had been patronizing this bar for half a century, but he wasn't the owner, and his pretend girlfriend was my age, so his only goal was to ensure I never came back. Because I realized what his true intentions were when I saw his reaction to her smiling at me, I made it my goal to flirt with her to provoke a reaction from him. The way I see our new tension is that he is now within my invisible energy field, and the emotional ball between us is yellow, representing the tension he caused. I knew if I kept flirting with her, the energy ball would turn red and shift toward him, causing him to curse me out and get kicked out of a bar he's spent thousands of dollars at. Every time she came near me, I spoke to her. About the third time, he raised his voice pretending to shout at the TV, but I knew it was his anger; that ball was moving toward his side. Then he started talking about his college team, so I began discussing my college team with her. At that point, he asked me what college I attended, so I told him where I went, then added that I did so while on Active Duty in the military. His aggressive tactics ended there as he paid and left while the bartender gave me her contact information. How did I win, you ask?

I don't need to win something I wasn't competing for; that's how I earn the admiration of the Bartender. When you compete, your invisible energy shield stays active because you're in a defensive mode, making it hard to know what energy balls are being aimed at you. Some say that lowering this shield makes you vulnerable to harm or exploitation. That's true. As I said earlier, no relationship is perfect—while we don't live in the darkest part of the Universe, we're still in a Dark Realm; thus, conflict is natural here. The only realm free of conflict is the Light Realm. Some call it Heaven, others Utopia, but the key point is that it's free from the negative emotions we face here. Living with positive emotions makes it easier to handle incoming emotions because you're effectively playing Offense and Defense, with the ability to redirect energy as needed.

Aesthetic Appreciation

Everything about your physical traits is perfect, as this is the only realm of thought you need to be in. Some of us like the vessel we're in, while others don't or want to make modifications; overall, it is a vessel for energy, either moving toward the Light or the Dark Realm.

That is all.

Amusement

I want to acknowledge my mother and credit her for shaping my understanding of 'Amusement.' Although she was strict during my childhood, she became very approachable as I grew older, which helped me work well with others. My mom never attended college, yet she built a career you'd hardly expect. Though she hasn't worked in years, she did a job similar to mine, despite lacking formal college training. She calls it a high-tech job, but when you think of high-tech careers, you don't usually picture hours of dealing with difficult coworkers. Instead, you imagine workplaces with sleeping pods and gourmet cafeterias designed more for comfort & collaboration.

I like to visit Glendale, CA, because it's one of those All-American Cities that embodies what other cities should aim to be, in my opinion. Glendale hosts many corporate offices for the entertainment industry, one of which is the Grand Central Creative Campus. When you drive by this building, you might not know exactly what it is, but you get that same feeling as if you're looking at an amusement park! This is a prime example of those positive vibes I mentioned earlier having a profound effect on a place.

I've lived in several cities across the United States, covering eight states, and I can genuinely say I've seen the full spectrum. Once, I stopped for gas in West Virginia, and if you were an alien that crash-landed on Earth in that state, the topography alone would astonish you. States like West Virginia, Mississippi, and others have the potential to be like Glendale; it just requires collective effort to shift from negative to positive energy.

Glendale was once a sundown town, where minorities weren't allowed after dark. I was told this by a girl I was dating. We visited the town a few times before she mentioned it. I noticed she was somewhat uneasy during our visits, but I didn't realize it was related to race until she brought it up. Before she mentioned it, I had never heard of a sundown town, but after looking it up, I learned it was a practice from over a hundred years ago. So, I wondered, why was it still relevant to her today if it happened so long ago?

If you're told not to go somewhere because you're not wanted there, it's best to respect that advice, even if your feelings feel different. I want to share a bit about my visit to a gas station in West Virginia, which was located in the Valley (Holler). I was on my way to see my brother in North Carolina, and when I stopped at another station for gas, I met a truck driver who remarked that I was lucky to get out of where I was, especially considering I'm black. The negative energy I sensed from him was stronger than anything I felt during my entire trip through West Virginia. It's important to remember that this man didn't even live in West Virginia; he seemed to be caught up in a mindset of perceived darkness—that's the difference between communities like Glendale and others.

Would you agree that an amusement park has the same or greater dangers than me visiting a town in West Virginia? I could most certainly get into a fight for looking at someone else's girl at an amusement park, the same as in any town in West Virginia, right? One might argue that yes, that's true, but we're talking about an amusement park full of safety protocols, families, smiles, and the fact that it's built for you to come and spend your money. I could counter that with several examples as we argue, but that's how the dark energy force starts—it manipulates feelings from the past to influence us here in the present.

My girlfriend and the truck driver were influenced by the same energy force that has trapped entire towns, states, and countries. Most of this influence didn't begin with some huge war from the past; it started with subtle statements like, "don't go over there, those folks don't like ya!" So, it somehow gets passed around and spirals into one group hating another as the dark energy particles spread like wildfire.

This type of wildfire has modernized itself as a dark energy evolutionary trait. For instance, if you're a struggling single, young, beautiful mother and post a video about needing help, you may get some assistance. But if you post another video and include the factor of race, you have now attracted the attention of the dark energy force. It seems that just talking about race online triggers higher engagement than topics like technology, math, or the sciences, which help society grow. Additionally, it's not like people aren't smart in these areas, but if the dark energy force has evolved to influence the algorithm, just know that these are the sales tactics of the dark energy force.

I won't lie and say I haven't fallen for these sales tactics myself. Recently, I came across a beautiful girl online who advocates for love within her white race and living in a society that's all white, but something about her makes me think she's doing what she can to keep her family financially secure. Talking about race seems to be helping her connect with her dedicated audience through affiliate marketing. I wonder if she'd still do this if her child had a disability or if she herself faced such challenges. We all get drawn to topics that spark raw emotions, but don't you think that if people are blind or missing a leg, they'd just want to go to an amusement park like anyone else? It seems that once you're influenced by dark energy, the toll on your health follows. That's why I focus my thoughts on positive feelings to maintain good health for myself and my descendants.

How many amusement park ads do you notice? Not many, right? Businesses target specific demographics in their marketing because it helps their sales strategies. It's almost as if they want us to think a certain way to keep everyone's mindset divided. For example, I mostly go to a gym with women because of my injuries, but when I first started, I sensed women were very aware I was there. I checked their ads, and every one featured both men and women, leading me to believe that since this gym offers lighter workouts with treadmills, it mainly attracts women, possibly because they have stronger lower bodies. Whether that was accurate or not, it was better than assuming all the women thought I wanted to date them, which might have become the reality and led to me being kicked out or canceling my membership.

At my gym, I cultivated an energy neural pathway through my positive emotional pool, aligning my thought process with like-minded individuals. Who are these people? Essentially, anyone I encounter, as the Light Realm forms experience pathways via the particles it transmits to guide us. This is why amusement parks, whether large or small, are universally recognized—they create a shared positive energy pathway for everyone present.

Awe

Have you ever been so amazed or impressed by something that it changed you? I remember moving to California in 2017 and being captivated by the palm trees. Even though I had lived in California for several years, the real change didn't occur until I was driving along Ventura Blvd in the Studio City neighborhood. It was the energetic vibe of that area that made me believe I could do anything if I kept a positive mindset. Before moving to Studio City, I lived in a town called Riverside, and although it's only 60 miles from Los Angeles proper, it felt like light-years away from my hopes of becoming something meaningful. Don't get me wrong, Riverside is a great place if that's where you want to be, but for anyone who moved to California from far away, you know that you're an outsider, and most outsiders get stuck somewhere they don't want to be if they lose sight.

When I first moved to Riverside, everything felt wonderful: I had a new job, a girlfriend, and a hopeful vision of settling down. My conscience was at peace, but as I started to change my long-term goals, my subconscious reflected my deeper feelings. You see, I was letting go of my ultimate dream to meet societal expectations at my age. People in their mid-30s often feel pressured to find a partner, settle down, buy a home, and have children, which can create a lot of internal and external pressure. My question for anyone feeling this way—whether they are applying these pressures to themselves or others—is how someone can pursue these milestones if they haven't yet experienced genuine, joyful feelings and a sense of wonder about the meaning of life. Maybe a better question is: how can we find harmony between our personal sense of purpose and societal expectations?

Thinking back to the moment I first drove onto Ventura Blvd brings a warm sense of awe in my heart. I knew deep down that this journey would guide me toward experiences that felt like working for the Light Realm Energy Force. The road to Ventura Blvd from Riverside wasn't smooth either. Just a few months before I made the move to Studio City, I faced losing my job. It's natural to feel overwhelmed by negative emotions during such times, and I wasn't immune to that either. On top of that, I received calls from people reminding me I was getting older without a marriage or children, while others asked if I was working in Hollywood—something I wasn't doing at that moment, feeling like my dreams were slipping away. But I've learned that when you draw strength from positive feelings and connect with the Light Realm, nothing can truly be over, because its energy is far more powerful than any dark force.

Both the Light and dark energy forces try to recruit you by stirring feelings of awe at certain milestones in this physical life cycle. I remember being in awe of a girl I met in Hollywood because she matched what I desired, both physically and mentally. However, during our first conversation, she introduced something that could cloud my thoughts about the Light Realm: sexual desire. Imagine feeling lonely for months, or maybe dating someone you're not attracted to, when suddenly the person of your dreams walks by and wants to be with you that night. That's exactly what happened. I thought maybe the Light Energy Force was offering me this chance because it saw the sacrifices I was making. Maybe this is the reward for keeping my thoughts positive. The bad news is, unfortunately, the dark energy force skillfully uses positive emotions to pull you in as well.

Meeting someone you truly desire usually provokes more positive than negative feelings. The same is true for places, experiences, or events you attend for the first time. The girl I was most attracted to had a job but never shared where she worked, which makes sense since it's none of my business. I asked if she enjoyed her job, and she said yes, but her energy seemed to fade, which I saw as a sense of emptiness. At that moment, I felt a connection because I had been asked the same question before losing my job and had responded with the same emptiness. Why do we lie in these situations? I believe it's because most people do what's necessary to survive. Even though she didn't tell me her occupation like I did, we were aligning with our subconscious.

People often tell me I resemble a military guy, which was my previous job, and for the most part, I don't see that as a bad thing, but this falls within their subconscious. What if I decided to be an astronaut? Do you think society will support this or marginalize me into what I should be? When do dreams expire? That's what I'd like to ask someone who thinks like this.

We really admire those who achieve great things early in life, but since no one knows their expiration date, there's no reason to give up or lose hope. Living in California for the past five years has shown me that many dreamers step onto Sunset Boulevard, just like others head back home when things don't go as planned. I've met inspiring people with big dreams, yet sometimes they find reasons to fit into the collective mindset. We just need to change our subconscious images of a CEO being an older Caucasian man, or Black people working as security guards, or even Asians doing our pedicure or excelling in math. These are just a few examples, but I truly believe that our subconscious biases have held us back from growing as a society.

The talent pool isn't confined to suburbs or Ivy League universities; it also encompasses the homeless asking for change, as this is where the full spectrum of human ideas converges!

Calmness

I remember my days filled with anger and anxiety, which others could sense, so they generally stayed away. However, I wasn't alone in that dark space. The dark energy force was always recruiting—people, objects, and places—to pull me further in. Around 2016, I moved to Arizona and decided to dedicate my energy fully to darkness, believing I had been wronged in life. Despite consciously choosing to turn away, I didn't realize my subconscious still gravitated toward the Light Realm, largely due to my mother's ingrained teachings. When I contemplated doing something negative, the fear of the consequences would dominate my actions. Just as the Dark Realm influences your path, so does the Light, and ironically, it was doing so more than ever. Eventually, I realized that the Light and Dark Realms are not separate paths; they are one and the same.

You don't need to physically travel by forging new paths with your thoughts; instead, you create neural connections that mirror the same feelings. These connections form highways within the particle realms of the Universe. It would be wonderful if I stepped outside and everyone was in a joyful mood, smiling all day because life is great. But what truly matters isn't the appearance of meanness—it's the conscious thought pool people draw from, which influences the collective subconscious energy. This type of energy appears to fuel the growth of dark energy forces. This, ladies and gentlemen, is the key to the Universe within you.

All these feelings fall into either the negative or positive experience pools. These experiences are often influenced by others' actions or recent events, with them leaning toward either the Light or the Dark Realm. For example, if we have around 45,000 thoughts daily and 95% are repetitive, our main concern should be how many steer us toward positivity. If 80% of our thoughts originate from the negative pool, it might seem more natural to react to conflict, since we're accustomed to it, living in the Dark Realm. The key is to recognize and openly acknowledge that we are in the Dark Realm, so we understand that conflict is an inevitable part of this state.

A close friend of mine shares daily spiritual messages, and I enjoyed them and found comfort in them for years. As I improved my life through positive thinking, I noticed I no longer felt that same peaceful calm feeling from his messages. One day, I reached out to him for general help with something I thought he could assist with. Instead of offering help, he said he couldn't and didn't even try. You might wonder what I asked for or why I still consider him a friend. At one point, he was there to help me when I was in a hole, but when I asked for help with my business, it raised questions. He saw me fired, living in my car, and now I was seeking his help for my business—his subconscious was battling between who I was and who I am. This reflects a larger societal issue where dark energy seems to be prevailing.

For many years, I lacked peace, causing my behavior to be far from calm. I began to find tranquility only after realizing I could choose which thought patterns to engage with. I used to wake up expecting the day to go poorly, and usually, that was indeed the case. However, when I shifted my mindset to believe that today would be great, my reality started reflecting that. I remember telling myself I would meet someone special, and eventually, I did! It felt like discovering a small version of myself in my mind's command center, where I started guiding my thoughts instead of simply reacting to emotional impulses. My music choices have also facilitated this process. Sometimes I listen only to the chorus, but more often, I focus on the chorus and lyrics. I can typically gauge the artist's emotional state based on how I feel from the lyrics, chorus, and beat combination. If the beat is catchy but the lyrics reveal they are being hated on, I recognize I'm in a negative thought pattern. Conversely, if the lyrics are positive but the beat makes me scowl at other drivers, it's not contributing to my calm.

Calmness is peace, and peace is only felt through experiencing it. Are you feeling peaceful with the people you interact with? What about the movies, music, or streaming content you engage in daily? Are they creating peace, or does their artistry seem to draw from negative emotions? Measuring your engagement with everyone against your feelings is the only way to understand where your energy vessel will end up.

Excitement

When I started expressing positive emotions, it showed physically in more smiles and an overall positive aura. However, since we live in a conflict realm, I experience energy clashes with random people almost every day. Many of my family members or close friends, who knew me as a despondent loner, tried to say or do things to pull me back into negative thought patterns. Negative patterns are low frequency, while positive ones are high; so even though they're next to each other, you have to ascend to reach the higher levels. If the higher levels are above, how can they clash with the lower ones? It's simple because you allow them to.

The world we live in today calls for excitement to be shared through photos and videos, but if you go out in public smiling at everyone and greeting strangers with a smile, people might think you're weird or even worse, very weak. Additionally, gender plays a role because women shouldn't show too much excitement, or else certain unfortunate events could happen. I encourage everyone reading this to understand that you can feel excited in the right place or at the right time, but the only place where it is acceptable to fully express your positive emotions without any ill intentions is in the Light Realm. This is where I strive to be, so I am excited to earn my spot there.

Interest

Words such as unity, attraction, and entertainment trigger shared thought patterns that lead to similar feelings and outcomes. Before adding the adverb 'good' or 'bad' before 'feeling,' did you realize that 'feeling' is more a verb than a noun? If you haven't realized this yet, an experience is an emotion or sensation that causes a physical reaction in your body—one that you can't always control. But what if you could control it? What if you could get punched in the face without feeling negative emotions afterward? And what if you could turn your fight response toward your coworker or that person at the gym, with whom you've been non-verbally beefing, into a feeling of close friendship?

As I've often noted, our universe is unfortunately filled with conflict, so I wouldn't recommend suddenly becoming lenient with someone you have issues with. Nonetheless, shared interests can lessen tension, especially when disagreement arises from a misunderstanding about a common experience. I remember a workout session where the person next to me was distracted by their phone. The instructor told them phones weren't permitted during the session. Knowing they were new, I mentioned that the instructor had given me a similar warning once, which created a moment that helped us bond. Despite this, the instructor and I became bitter rivals, with this person becoming my "Top Energy Opp." Whenever I saw them, I used body language to show my disdain, and they responded in kind. I grew to dislike them so much that I took pleasure in showing disrespect to gain the upper hand. It was only during a group celebration that included other instructors for a shared workout goal that I realized I needed to reconsider my feelings.

During our group workout, we aimed for specific goals, which was quite challenging. When we finally finished, everyone cheered, except for my "Top Energy Opp," which not only ruined the moment for me but also affected the whole group. The acting instructor noticed the negative vibe and allowed us to talk about it near the end. We had faced a similar situation before, but I had previously chosen not to join the open discussion. That day, I felt I needed to speak because the instructor's attitude toward me was affecting me negatively. As I mentioned earlier about feelings as actions, this particular emotion was fueling negative thoughts, and the dark energy force was influencing us toward its own goal.

The path to achieving anything starts with a positive thought, which can grow into a collective feeling of positivity shared by others. However, for this to happen, you need to recognize conflicting energies so that everyone can share a sense of victory. Our team rarely truly succeeded because the feeling of achievement did not spread throughout the room, as two out of 20 people didn't share the same positive mindset. Have you faced this at work? Sadly, similar issues occur with larger projects like business deals, globalization efforts, and creative projects. Success stories are uncommon because energy clashes often cause failure, as the Instructor and I have experienced.

What I appreciate about shared interest is its ability to help conflicting parties find common ground, enabling them to work toward shared goals. For example, during the Cold War, members of the U.S. Atomic Commission, unlikely to be social media friends, recognized that producing their project first was crucial; without it, the free world we enjoy today might resemble authoritarian regimes.

If someone says or does actions you don't like and you can't find any shared interest, the Universe has made it that way, and it's best to move on from that person, place, or thing. Sometimes, it's not that you're bad or they're bad; it's just how the invisible particles of pathways work for the Universe. I was looking through my phone's contacts and found several people I used to spend time with, but I don't know what they're doing in life. However, with everyone one of them, I felt they were good, and as long as the good feeling is there when I think of them, I know that's the Universe letting me know we'll see each other in the Light Realm when it's all said and done.

Sharing interests is a great way to make lifelong friends, but it's also important to remember that even if you don't share interests with certain individuals or groups, appreciating who they are is essential to staying aligned with the Light Energy Force. I once met a Hispanic guy who told me he knew a very influential social media family, but I had no idea who they were, and he was surprised.

Instead of making a silly remark like "I'm black, how would I know these people,' I asked him to send me a video. That simple act of appreciation kept us friends today. There are millions of entertainers, artists, influencers, and others with huge followings. Even if you're not one of them, acknowledging someone else's interests can create positive subatomic particles or vibes between you and others from any background.

Joy

It's painful to admit, but this is the hardest part for me to write because feeling joy is difficult to access intentionally, especially since we live in a conflicted or Dark Realm. I've spent many weekends alone and isolated because I know my mind works against the idea of friendship, relationships, and basic social needs. Even as I write this, I can't think of more than five people who would be at my wedding, which doesn't bring me closer to the Light Realm. I often have dreams where people I grew up with or know are upset with me for not engaging enough with them. These are not pleasant dreams, as I often wake up feeling disappointed that I let it come to this.

These dreams indicate that lacking relationships or human connections impacts my subconscious, even though my conscious mind attributes it to being an artist. But how can I be an artist without engaging with human emotions? I think this is why I struggle as an artist — I avoid these connections to sidestep judgment. As a child, I often felt despondent, but when religious individuals influenced me, my conscience and subconscious focused on actions that the Creator would approve of. This led to the belief that true joy would only be experienced in the Light Realm.

I became so immersed in following religious rules that I believed anyone not adhering to them couldn't have a relationship with me. I often missed events, fearing sinful activities based on my thoughts in my conscious mind. Reflecting on these missed experiences, I feel sadness, which could have turned into joy if I hadn't been so bound by religious restrictions. I recall a close friend inviting me to several parties where people were smoking, but I always declined. Interestingly, I liked a girl who was friends with someone attending those parties, and I later discovered she had asked if I would be there, missing a potential love connection. Some religious individuals might say it wasn't meant to be, but they overlook that true love reveals joy, something they can't help you find.

Some might say you don't need love to feel joy, but I've been in love, and it's the greatest happiness anyone can experience. Love doesn't come easily, though; you must find purpose within yourself before you can truly love, which involves creating a sense of meaning in your life. I once met a guy who loved working on trains;

he explained everything about them to me and met his wife during one of his early jobs—this is someone who found joy but is also navigating through this conflict realm toward the Light. Another person worked at a retail store selling merchandise and loved her job because she got to talk to different people each day. She also wore a very large diamond ring on her wedding finger, and her aura was the same as the train guy's.

While browsing my visual or audio content, I tend to focus on positive topics because I know my goals. One video featured a well-known TV personality dancing with her kids to my favorite singer's song, with the singer making a surprise appearance. I've watched that scene hundreds of times! Later, I researched her background and discovered she has made significant progress since the incident that brought her fame. Now, she is a billionaire entrepreneur, mother, philanthropist, and uses her platform to support the wrongly convicted. Despite her success, her unresolved love story continues to captivate viewers. Interestingly, she rose to fame after a privately recorded video leaked and went viral online, turning her into a household name.

She could have allowed that public incident to define her, but instead, she leveraged the publicity by launching her businesses. I think her mother's way of demonstrating resilience against public scrutiny was through creating value with a reality TV show, and it succeeded. It was so effective that reality TV became the highest revenue-generating form of viewership across all media. This illustrates that even if a negative emotion dominates, the Universe can reinterpret it, recognizing your overall actions and intentions.

It's clear she found happiness in her understanding of life, so I'm confident she'll find love again. What matters most is that she maintains a positive mindset. I have no problem with anyone, including religious folks, being in any mindset, but my question to you is: do you truly feel like you're drawing from the pool of positive emotions? Better yet, can you imagine a place where joy exists alongside everyone?

Over the years, I've naturally adopted an extrovert persona. When I attend social gatherings, I enjoy engaging or simply observing others happily interacting. If I don't experience this, I leave feeling disappointed, believing I didn't energize the crowd enough for everyone's enjoyment. As an acting extrovert, I know I'll be talked about in small groups, but I don't mind since I rarely see the same people at different events. My relaxed attitude about not always wanting to attend the same social settings actually masks my fear of judgment, which I now realize is influenced by the dark energy force.

Choosing to steer clear of the dark energy force means being open to the insights of Light Realm seekers, who might share their thoughts about me. However, I find that the happiness these connections bring far exceeds any feelings of emptiness or loneliness. Am I headed to smoker parties now? I'm not sure yet. But if it feels right—like I'm truly drawing from a well of positive emotions—then I'll gladly go with that flow.

Nostalgia

I want you to review the lists below and consider which key emotions from your childhood have shaped who you are today.

Positive	Negative
Admiration	Anger
Adoration	Anxiety
Aesthetic/Appreciation	Awkwardness
Amusement	Boredom
Awe	Confusion
Calmness	Craving
Empathic Pain	Disgust
Excitement	Entrancement
Interest	Fear
Joy	Horror

Nostalgia   Sadness

Relief   Sexual Desire

Romance

Satisfaction

Surprise

Relief

This is one of those emotions that withstands a period when feelings like stress and anxiety seem to keep you in a dark tunnel. Nonetheless, by focusing on the idea of a light at the end of the tunnel, it can be the most rewarding positive emotion of all.

One of the best ways I gauge which energy force I'm subconsciously in is by recounting recent dreams. I once had a dream where I was walking with friends I didn't know, in a town I'd never been to, and something told me to look at the sky; there was nothing there. I then looked back at these friends, looked up again, and the sky was full of alien aircraft. One aircraft performed an aerial combat technique, and fear consumed me. None of my friends seemed to be looking at the sky, so I ran, and they followed me.

Why did I have this kind of dream? In real life, I aspired to be someone no one mentioned or noticed—someone who would one day work on films. I often think about this dream because I wonder why I was the only one who seemed to notice thousands of foreign objects in the sky. Was it because I was the only one who could see them, or was I the first to see them appear in the sky? This could be true because later on in that dream, those friends and I were hiding from their ongoing arsenal attack, so I assume no one was looking up.

The core element in all my dreams is my age; I tend to be much younger in them. To understand my subconscious feelings better, I viewed this dream as symbolizing my life surrounded by unfamiliar people in a strange yet recognizable place, facing an unknown adversary. All these conscious emotions reflected my mix of fear. I realized that upon waking, and I chose to confront this by accepting it as a natural emotion, while also consciously telling myself to shift away from this negative thought pattern. Since I appear younger in these dreams, I know it's not actually me, but another version acting out the fear within.

Your negative thoughts secretly pretend to be you because they want to work for the dark energy force to take your energy permanently. The scenes, visual scenarios, and overall productions in your dreams are a ploy to keep your mind in that dark tunnel. Here's the thing: even though you can't control these unsolicited horror films they're putting on for you, the only thing you need to know is why it's happening.

The dark energy force isn't the only entity creating these original short films for you; The Light Realm is also doing the same. One of the best dreams I've ever had was learning how to fly. To me, this was around the time I realized I wanted to be a Writer, so learning how to fly represented a new freedom I was beginning to explore. Years later, I had the Alien attack dream, and it mostly represented my fear of producing films, which I am currently in the process of doing.

It's a great relief to have written this book, but I'll go over that more at the end. I think the best relief for you is knowing you're a few pages away from finishing this book, so congratulations. It's been a long and hopefully engaging journey, so you're almost there, friend.

Romance

This will be my favorite section because I've realized that sexual self-discipline begins with lessons of Romance. I believe it might be helpful to fully outline these steps so you can better understand what I mean, but also keep in mind that your thought patterns are closely linked to your feelings.

1. Take charge of your sexual desire.

2. The end.

That's it! There's no formula or way to control your feelings when you see someone you're attracted to because, honestly, you don't know who you'll be attracted to until you meet them. The control comes with your thinking.

I once met a girl at a restaurant who looked like an exotic social media model; I was instantly attracted to her. I approached her, and all the good vibes were there, so I got her number and had the smart idea to ask her to hook up. She wanted to hook up, but it cost me more than money because now that I was solely focused on sexual desire, it was subconsciously affecting my sense of purpose.

To all those whose competitive instincts flare up when meeting someone with a lot of money or who feel they are more attractive than you, and who find non-verbal ways to dismiss them, understand that you don't have to compete when you're on a path of purpose or meaning. American filmmaker George Lucas found a creative way to show the world through film how the forces of the Light and Dark Realms work, so the Universe made sure he had love in his personal life before we knew him as HIM.

If George Lucas decided to go to a nightclub to find a woman, what do you think would happen if he wanted the same person as you? His advantage isn't about his net worth or his looks; it's because he found meaning in a skill he loves to do and overcame several obstacles to bring it to life. This, ladies and gentlemen, is the science of business and a sure way the Universe will provide you with love.

I used to go to nightclubs hoping to meet a girl, but I always ended up at home alone. Why? Because many women go out just to have fun. When I started going out with the intention to have fun myself, after spending all week stuck in my head, focused on feelings of meaning, it was like they could sense my true intentions. So, at least, they wanted to know who I really was.

You become an interesting person when you start diligently working on things that interest you. Once you're in this kind of mental space, romance becomes easier because you have something to talk about with someone you also desire sexually. The feelings of sexual desire happen involuntarily, and others may feel the same, so you might face competition. But then, it's time to showcase your romance skills.

Romance is discussed in books, movies, plays, office watercooler talks—you name it. But you really need to tailor it to the person you like to elevate yourself above the competition, akin to rising above the chaos. Doesn't this kind of elevation sound familiar?

At the start of this book, I likened the positive emotional pool to the sky, while the negative pool is more akin to roads. I made this comparison to highlight that when two people lack meaningful goals or share similar thought patterns leading to many of the same destinations, they tend to compete and endure the negative emotions experienced while driving. Conversely, pilots control their flight plans, have more defined routes, and arrive at their destinations feeling free.

Although pilots are not competing like car drivers, they still need to consider the environment. Even if we try to hide it, the Universe knows which emotional pool we're drawing from because it acts as a repository for the conflict between the Light and dark energy forces. Like the weather in our environment, it sends various changes as if redirecting our subconscious pathways based on our collective emotional thought pool. In fact, entire groups can be on the same thought paths heading in different directions, but the way to know where their subconscious is observing environmental factors.

I lived in a lot of places, each for a few months or several years. For the ones I stayed several years with, it was because of the genuine love they showed each other and the love they earned from me. On the other hand, I lived in places where they were extremely nice, but their surface-level love and what they do often translate into a negative emotional environment, especially in business.

When someone embarks on a quest to discover a skill they love, they will eventually want to share it, creating demand. This demand leads to profit, which helps stabilize their livelihood. With a stable life, their emotions also stabilize, bringing love. Consider a movie where the main character starts off totally disoriented but finds their purpose by the end. Usually, there's a love interest who witnesses their obstacles and is inspired to give themselves fully to the main character because of their successful journey. This narrative reflects how the Universe monitors our energy struggles.

Growing up in a low-income, impoverished neighborhood, the dominant mindset was often centered around gangs and hostility toward rivals. Even when we visited the nicer side where everything looked better and smelled sweeter, I could still sense the underlying aggression — it was just less obvious, but these negative energies from dark forces still influenced them just as they influenced us, only in a different form. So, what does all of this have to do with romance?

Some of my closest friends from that low-income, impoverished area changed their aggressive behavior once they met someone they truly liked, including myself. Romance inspires actions driven by love, placing you in the highest vibrational state of the positive emotional spectrum since love includes all these emotions. Most importantly, it provides the real-time experience of being in love, making you feel free and soaring like pilots, rather than stuck in congested, delayed traffic lanes below.

Engaging in romantic thoughts about someone you're interested in or already with helps keep you aligned with the Light Energy Force. If you don't focus on living your life predominantly in this thought pattern, the dark energy force considers it a success and may engulf you in darkness.

Understanding how the dark energy force gauges your emotions is very tricky, especially if you've been given what seems like a harder life than others. At one point in my life, I was completely abstinent, so my sexual drive was at its peak. My conscience told me I was doing good, but my feelings were tied to a negative pool. I was angry all the time, and for some strange reason, I was getting rejected more than when I was practicing "self-love."

Romance is much more difficult than exploring your sexual desires freely because it takes a long time to find out if love is mutual. Romance requires patience, and patience is a skill that demonstrates self-discipline—something I had to learn the hard way.

As a younger man, most of my friends encouraged romance by teasing each other and building confidence to pursue the girl we liked. It wasn't until I found out that the girl I liked slept with the most popular guy that I started to question romance.

When I reached my mid-twenties, I wanted to have more sex, but I also wanted to do it the right way—get married. Being in the military at the time, it seemed very easy to get married but extremely hard to find love, especially since I often used romantic techniques. Because I was both in the military and young, this was seen as weak by the women I was trying to court.

Back then, I believed women should see me as someone interested in shared interests and intellectual ideas to build friendships before considering dating. I understood that dark energy would consume every subatomic particle in my brain if I kept myself in a certain thought lane, believing that people subconsciously see me as an ultra-masculine, hypersensitive being. I was wrong to think like that because I still wasn't considering my purpose, which, combined with my self-discipline, would have allowed me to elevate to a higher frequency much sooner. If you don't know this by now, it's time: good people exist at a higher frequency, and that's where you'll find your person.

What I discovered was that I wasn't weak for trying out romantic techniques; I was just trying them at the wrong frequency. I once dated an exotic dancer, and what I remember most is her attraction to my intellectual capability. I remember we were watching something on television when a video came up of a place, Jerusalem, but they hadn't said it. When I said it, she replied, "You're so smart, how did you know that?" Afterwards, she was hinting at wanting to have kids with a smart man so they could be smart.

Exotic dancers often face some of the most aggressive and hypersexual men. However, the fact that she wanted to have children with me, based on my advanced thought process, is the clearest proof that a versatile romantic individual can get what they want. It wasn't about me being smart; it was about taking the time to understand a topic outside my perceived norm enough for her and me to discuss, instead of engaging in trendy conversations. From that moment, I realized that trying to influence the subconscious minds of millions was too overwhelming. Instead, focusing on my own thought process was the only way to develop healthier subconscious patterns.

Dating someone based on aspects like race or physical appearance alone is permissible within the dark energy force because it aligns with the desire-driven mindset, where aggression and competition are dominant. However, if you connect with someone through positive emotions, a non-competitive romantic bond is likely to form. This happens because your subatomic energy field and theirs are naturally aligning through subconscious channels involving shared interests, values, and beliefs. It will feel as if you've experienced the same countless moments but only recently subconsciously crossed paths, once the Universe has fulfilled its purpose for your meeting.

Satisfaction

Have you ever heard of Magnum Opus? For an artist or writer, this is essentially their greatest work, but I'd like you to take this word and apply it to your life. If someone stopped and asked you what you are known for, would you have an answer? Would you create something, or would you feel incensed they had the nerve to ask you?

My mother is proud of raising her four sons, and when people ask about or allude to her life, she refers to us as her greatest achievement. She never attended college and raised us alone with the help of government subsidies, but she was able to find purpose. Everyone is meant for something, and no one is a mistake. The dark energy force's trick is to trap you in a state of unfulfilling actions, which is why we see substance abuse and homelessness increasing today, rather than the realization of creative ideas. Having an idea is having meaning, and that is the pursuit of satisfaction. Being satisfied is a feeling we can all work toward and negotiate with each other to achieve.

Surprise

One of the best things about writing this book is knowing that I consciously chose love over the hate I once felt for many things I thought the Creator ignored me on. The scars on my chest from Gynecomastia surgery make me feel embarrassed to take my shirt off. When I think about all the guys at the beach who were born with flat chests, jealousy creeps in. If I dwell too much on these same guys with hair, hate for the Creator arises.

If I hadn't been burdened with those two ailments I just mentioned, maybe I'd accept this life more. Maybe I wouldn't care about the conflict of the Light and dark energy forces recruiting me, but maybe I live in an unknown Universe. These two flaws have created conundrums between choosing greatness or hatred. As I measure my life against these pools, I feel as though I'm more than sixty percent positive emotions. I say this because aggression still lingers within. I probably get into slight confrontations two times a month with random people, but I think about it forty percent of the time. For example, I recently got into it with A foreign guy over something minor. I was in a mindset thinking this person felt they were better than me, while also feeling rejected by a foreign girl, so the dark energy force saw an opening, and I happily let it in.

Negative emotions will come to us, but do we really want to end up sharing a public toilet for years? You see, I don't fear death, but I do fear using the toilet in front of a stranger with no walls. I know this sounds abstract, but the feeling of losing something like bathroom privacy can help you stay in a positive emotional space.

My mother and I once talked about how I died as an infant and was revived by a woman who lives in her building. She told me that when the woman revived me from suffocating on her couch, she died shortly afterward. Ironically, when I'm walking down the street or drawing from the negative pool, a darker-skinned woman dressed in a white nurse's outfit appears in my dreams. When I told my mother in detail about this woman—about my dreams—she said that she was the woman who revived me as a baby. You can call them angels, God, Allah, Buddha, or simply the Universe, but something out there is measuring the energy within us that doesn't need to sleep and moves through our dreams.

Last Words

This is written for the person who picks up this book seeking a brief overview or flips to the back for a summary after reading a few lines. Before I continue, I want to clarify that I never intended to become an author, nor do I see writing as a lifelong career. I wrote this book because I felt something was broken in my mind as I was losing hope. It helped me understand why homeless people often talk to themselves on the street. Writing this has recalibrated my mind to function better, and I hope it can do the same for you if your brain needs recalibration. I imagined taking my brain out, cleaning it of impurities, and reinserting it to refresh my perspective on life.

I'm here to explain that although the Universe oversees the conflict between Dark and Light Energy Forces, ultimately, the dark energy force will prevail in destroying all but one Light source in the Universe—it's only a matter of time. It feeds off our collective negative energy and dispatches its vast subatomic particles to induce more negative drivers like competition and aggression among humans, aiming to eliminate all Light from the Universe.

For everyone reading this, I commend you for choosing to read instead of scrolling through social media because you are not only strengthening your brain through neuroplasticity, but you're also connecting your subconscious mind to experiences beyond those dictated by the social media algorithm.

Algorithms have been helpful, but as I mentioned in chapter 7, they can also lead us into groupthink. Reflecting on how the term "entrancement" appears in both negative and positive contexts has made me realize how the dark energy force has evolved over the centuries. It has used racism, sexism, hatred, and similar tactics to continue expanding its influence.

The world has struggled with slavery and racism throughout history. Despite progress in some areas, others remain stuck in the past. I believe this is influenced by a dark energy force. For example, when a social media influencer focuses on empowering their own race but shares videos that demean others, it's a tactic of this dark energy. Similarly, when algorithms favor sensational or sexual content over educational material, it reflects this force's particles overwhelming our minds at an alarming rate. The same dark energy that fueled slavery in ancient times still tries to recruit us through algorithms today; it has simply metamorphosed, but I'm here to make you aware!

Throughout this book, the term "dark energy force" is not capitalized to diminish its power, while Light Energy Force is capitalized to highlight our hopefully shared goal. I didn't write this as a Black man with a hidden agenda; I wrote it so that you and I can find ways to honor our differences and ensure our energy vessels reach the Light Realm, where negative emotions cannot exist.

The key takeaway from all of this is to imagine the sun's rays shining down on you, but there's no heat, and you can't see the sun. Are those rays, or subatomic particles, as I called them throughout this book, bright or dark? Better yet, if someone drew a stick figure of you right now, would you be light-filled or dark-filled? If you know the answer to that, then maybe this book isn't for you. But if you're not sure and also feel like you need to wash your brain of impurities, it's time to walk on this journey with me. See you where the end meets the beginning!